AF398337

Martin Reén

Sonship, Faith and Vision

Pioneering the Love of the Father

Proofreading: Marie Enoksson
Publishing House : Healing Streams
Print: BoD – Books on Demand, Norderstedt, Germany
ISBN: 978-91-527-8896-7

Table of Contents

PREFACE

This is my fourth and probably final book in the series that I've chosen to call *Abiding in the Love of God*. The vision for this book was birthed in my heart during a one-week seminar, where some good friends and I taught a group of wonderful lovers of Jesus. All of them carried a strong calling to be creative pioneers. It was a very exciting week filled with anointed teaching and powerful times of ministry with a lot of impartation and prophetic prayers. At that time, I had just finished my earlier book, *The Burning Love of Jesus Christ*, so I was a little bit hesitant to start writing another book so soon. But as soon as the first day of this short-term school had started, this book was downloaded into my spirit.

This book is all about how being rooted and grounded in the love of the Father raises us up to live in the inheritance and blessings of our sonship. We belong to the royal family of Jesus, which has received the glorious mandate from our blessed Father to spread His love by establishing His Kingdom everywhere. We can move forward with this endeavor in bold faith, while we're living out of our sonship and identity in Christ:

"I speak to you eternal truth. The Son is unable to do anything from himself or through his own initiative. I only do the works that I see the Father doing, for the Son does the same works as his Father. "Because the Father loves his Son so much, he always reveals to him everything that he is about to do. And you will all be amazed when he shows him even greater works than what you've seen so far" (John 5:19-20 TPT).

Jesus never acted on His own initiative. His ministry flowed out of His relationship with His Father. Jesus only did what He saw the Father do and the Father always revealed everything He did to Jesus. Since we are sons and daughters, we are called into a similar relationship with our Father.

This means that we are called to live a lifestyle of revelation and vision where we walk in the overcoming faith of Jesus Christ, as the manifested sons of God. This is the reason that I have chosen to call this book: *Sonship, Faith and Vision — Pioneering the Love of the Father*. As we're abiding in His love, we will be compelled to take a journey of faith, so that we can live in the fullness of the Father's purposes for us. This book is meant to encourage you during this journey into the Father's heart. My hope and prayers are that this book will provide both hope, inspiration and a lot of revelation from Jesus!

Your brother in Christ,
Martin Reén

INTRODUCTION

When you see the ark of the covenant of the Lord your God with the Levitical priests carrying it, then you shall set out from your place and go after it. However, there shall be a distance between you and it of about two thousand cubits by measurement. Do not come near it, so that you may know the way by which you shall go, for you have not passed this way before (Jos. 3:3-4 NASB).

Usually, when believers think of the love of the Father, they think of it as an inner-healing message. Since we will find both healing and restoration in His love, they're right in doing so, but there is much more to knowing His love than just being healed. There is a wild and unpredictable element to His love. It delivers us from bondages, it shatters chains and breaks us out of religious boxes. His love could never be contained in the box of human traditions or be held captive by a religious system. The love of the Father will renew the mind and reform the heart of every person who drinks from it. Therefore, it raises up believers who break out of spiritual poverty and dry traditions, so that they can find a new way of walking with the Father and living out the life of Christ. Being filled with the wild love of God will cause us to walk in ways where we have not traveled before.

Why I Wrote This Book

The title of this book is *Sonship, Faith and Vision — Pioneering the Love of the Father*. This is the fourth book in a series on the love of God and it builds a lot on the truths laid out in the three previous books:

- *Abiding in the Father's love*
- *Partnering with the Love of Christ*
- *The Burning Love of Jesus Christ*

I recommend that you read those books as well. Doing that will provide a fuller picture of the love of God for you. I have written this book to highlight an important and a very exciting aspect of the Father's love, which is the unpredictable and wild side of His love. Jesus said:

For God so loved the world, that He gave His only Son, so that everyone who believes in Him will not perish, but have eternal life. For God did not send the Son into the world to judge the world, but so that the world might be saved through Him (John 3:16-17 NASB).

By making this statement, Jesus reveals that our Father will never give up and that He is doing everything He can to save and heal as many as possible. He is very creative in finding ways to reach this goal. The Father's motivation in everything that He is doing is love and He wants to fill us with His love. When that happens, our hearts will be transformed and we will start to look at reality through God's eyes and dream His dreams. This will cause us to be possibility thinkers that tap into the full creativity of heaven. That is the only way that we can find new creative ways to reach the world with the gospel and to extend the Kingdom of God on this earth. That is what this book is all about.

Breaking Out of Religious Boxes

As we learn to abide in His love as a lifestyle, we will be renewed and transformed. This will create a longing within our hearts to break out of religious limitations and meaningless traditions that have held us back, so that we instead can pursue the visions and purposes of Jesus. Abraham is our example in this journey.

By faith Abraham, when he was called, obeyed by going out to a place which he was to receive for an inheritance; and he left, not knowing where he was going. By faith he lived as a stranger in the land of promise, as in a foreign land, living in tents with Isaac and Jacob, fellow heirs of the same promise; for he was looking for the city which has foundations, whose architect and builder is God (Hebr. 11.8-10 NASB).

Just like Abraham, we will be compelled to leave our old familiar territory to travel to the promised land. This is a journey of faith, where we will often find ourselves not really knowing where we are going. Our lifestyle will not match the expectation created by the religious world, concerning how a good believer is supposed to live and act. We will become a peculiar people who are filled with the love of Christ. We will be reflecting the unpredictable, wild nature of that love in even greater ways (2 Cor. 5:14).

Pioneering Lovers

It is more than obvious that God is raising up believers, whose lives have been transformed by the love and grace of the Father. The old way of living the Christian life and doing church will not work for these people. They will become pioneers and reformers who are longing for new expressions of their life with Christ and Kingdom living. Like Joshua, they will be traveling paths where they have not traveled before. It might sometimes look like these people really don't know where they are going, but they are led by the Holy Spirit. They are lovers of Jesus, who will not give up until they have reached their promised land. I assume that you're reading this book because you are one of them. My purpose with writing this book is to encourage you on this journey.

The Structure of This Book

This book consists of two parts. In the first part of this book, we are going to look at some general biblical principles of how to live out our sonship by walking in heavenly vision in bold faith. In the second part of this book, we will study the life of Abraham and Sarah, who are the spiritual parents of our faith. Their life provides a pattern for the believers who have been captured by a heavenly vision. Their story is a prophetic blueprint for all of us who feel compelled to leave our old, religious life to embrace the Father's purposes for us. The history of the people of God has been shaped by lovers of God, who have been totally captivated by a heavenly vision. They could not give up on their vision but were driven to see it fulfilled. By pursuing what they have seen, they shaped history and gave us a rich inheritance of blessings. Abraham is a primary example of such a man.

The Activations

At the end of each chapter, you'll find a section called *Activations*. The activations are there to provide a practical application to the teaching. You will get much more out of this book if you do these activations. They will help you to interact with the Holy Spirit to gain more revelation on the topic presented within each chapter. The activations are easy to work with and they will inspire you to grow in intimacy with Jesus Christ. These activations involve journaling, so I suggest that you have your electronic device or a notebook within reach while reading this book. In the Kingdom of God, we learn best by applying what we see. I believe the activations will be both helpful and fun as you interact with the Holy Spirit.

It has been a joy, but also a healthy challenge for me to write this book. The process of writing has challenged me to allow His love to bring reformation and a deeper transformation in my heart. It is more than obvious to me that the Father is leading us to places in the spirit, where we have not gone before. I'm not sure what that will look like, but I do know that it is going to be better than we could ever have imagined. Our future is indeed very exciting! I sincerely hope that you will be just as encouraged and blessed by reading this book as I have been by writing it.

Part 1: Sonship and Vision

In this part of the book, we will look at New Covenant ministry and how our calling flows out of sonship and identity in Christ. Knowing who we are will empower us to live in bold faith as we build the heavenly vision. We will discover how the revelation of who we are as children of God fits together with brokenness and humility before Jesus. Finally, we're going to look at how the essence of ministry is Christ expressing His own life through us. It is such an adventure to live out our sonship and to bear lasting fruit that glorifies the Father. A fruitful life of restful increase is built on our revelation of the Father's heart and our identity in Christ.

CHAPTER 1: A REVELATION OF JESUS CHRIST

Everything of true value in the Kingdom of God, will always be born from a revelation of the Father's heart. Growing in the love of the Father opens our eyes, so that we can receive more clarity and revelation of Him. When the Father reveals new things about Himself, our perspective of reality changes, which in turn creates a longing within our hearts to find new ways to respond to Him. Revelation stirs a deep and holy dissatisfaction in our hearts, by causing us to realize that God has so much more in store for us than we have yet experienced. When reading the gospels and the book of Acts, we can see how encounters with Jesus transformed people's lives all the time. Whenever someone had an encounter with Him that person couldn't return to their old life anymore. They were forever gloriously ruined by His grace.

Religious Terrorist Transformed into a Pioneering Missionary

The conversion of the apostle Paul is a powerful example of this. He was on his way to the city of Damascus to persecute and wipe out the church there. He had received a mandate from the high priest to arrest every believer he could find in Damascus and to bring them back to the religious council in Jerusalem, bound and in chains (Acts 9:1-2). Paul was totally convinced that he did the right thing. After all, he knew the Old Testament scriptures by heart and he was sure that the followers of Jesus had been badly deceived. In his mind, their very existence was a great threat to the existence of the Jewish people. But then Paul had a revelation of Jesus that changed everything. Let's read about this encounter in Paul's own words:

"As I was on the road, approaching Damascus about noon, a very bright light from heaven suddenly shone down around me. I fell to the ground

and heard a voice saying to me, 'Saul, Saul, why are you persecuting me?' "'Who are you, lord?' I asked. "And the voice replied, 'I am Jesus the Nazarene, the one you are persecuting.' The people with me saw the light but didn't understand the voice speaking to me" (Acts 22:6-9 NLT).

As Paul encountered the risen Jesus, he quickly realized that his old way of looking at life, as well as his own perspective about God and the Scriptures needed some serious update! It became obvious to Paul that he was the one who had been deceived, but through a revelation of Jesus he was now being set free. As Paul realized that he had been playing for the wrong team, he asked the Lord for help:

"And I said, 'What shall I do, Lord?' And the Lord said to me, 'Get up and go on into Damascus and there you will be told about everything that has been appointed for you to do.' But since I could not see because of the brightness of that light, I came into Damascus being led by the hand by those who were with me" (Acts 22:10-11 NASB).

The same light that had blinded his natural sight, enlightened his heart and gave him spiritual sight. The apostle Paul serves as a great example of how revelation changes our hearts. Of course, revelation usually do not come to us in this dramatic fashion, but the results will always be the same. When revelation illuminates our hearts, our perspective on both Jesus and our own lives will change dramatically. Revelation will compel us to break out into new territories with God.

Encountering Him Changes Us

As Paul was being led into the city of Damascus, he was blinded by the radiant light of Jesus Himself. This was a very humbling experience for Paul, but Jesus didn't want him to be stuck in that place for long. Jesus spoke to Ananias, one of the disciples who was a part of the body of Christ in Damascus and He sent him to minister to Paul. When Ananias prayed for Paul, he received his sight and was no longer blind (Acts 22:12-13). After Ananias had finished praying for Paul, he gave a prophetic word:

"And he said, 'The God of our fathers has appointed you to know His will and to see the Righteous One and to hear a message from His mouth. For you will be a witness for Him to all people of what you have seen and heard. Now why do you delay? Get up and be baptized and wash away your sins by calling on His name'" (Acts 22:14-16 NASB).

When we receive revelation from heaven, God will not leave us on our own to figure out what it means and how to apply it. Jesus will either show it to us directly, or He will send other believers to help us. Paul received a prophetic word that would carry him for the rest of his life. This gave Paul new direction and it set him on a path that would transform him into a pioneering apostle. We need to learn how to receive the people that God sends into our lives, as the amazing gifts that they truly are. Jesus primarily ministers to us through His body.

Paul fled from Damascus to escape the religious Jews there. They now saw Paul as a traitor and wanted to kill him. Paul returned to Jerusalem and as he was praying in the temple, Jesus spoke to him again. He revealed to Paul that he would not be received in Jerusalem. Instead, Jesus sent him to preach among the gentiles. *"Then the Lord said to me, 'Go; I will send you far away to the Gentiles"* *(Acts 22:21 NIV).* This redirected Paul's life in a radical way. He had been trained to think like a religious Jew, but this calling was the total opposite of the worldview of the Jewish people, at that time. This was obvious by the rage his testimony provoked in the religious people from Jerusalem (Acts 22:22-24). Revelation from God transformed Paul's life forever, from a religious terrorist into a pioneering apostle.

Revelation Reshapes our Lives

Revelation will always reshape our lives and fill us with dreams and visions from God. Revelation is never given just to provide information, but to impart new life from God into our spirits. It brings transformation, so that we can live the life that our Father has prepared for us. This is the reason that the true pioneers and reformers are always born through a renewed revelation of the heart of the Father. We don't have to try to become pioneers and reformers. We should instead ask the Father for a much deeper revelation of who He is. Knowing Him deeper will lead us on the path to find new ways to extend the Kingdom.

Revelation Reforms the Heart

All renewal and reformation always start within the heart of the believer. Before our minds can be renewed, the Holy Spirit need to enlighten our hearts. This is the reason that Paul is praying for the Ephesian church:

"…that the God of our Lord Jesus Christ, the Father of glory, may give to you the spirit of wisdom and revelation in the knowledge of Him, the eyes of your understanding being enlightened; that you may know what is the hope of His calling, what are the riches of the glory of His inheritance in the saints and what is the exceeding greatness of His power toward us who believe" (Eph. 1:17-19 NKJV).

A heart that is illuminated by revelation on the Father's love will be transformed. This is always a work of grace. Transformation in the Kingdom of God could never be accomplished through the strength of the flesh or simple willpower. The enlightenment that we receive by the Holy Spirit transforms us. It is a work of grace. Sometimes we might be tempted to act outside God's timing, by trying to bring about change by our own strength, but that will never produce any good fruit. We must learn to trust the grace of God to transform our lives.

In our ministry, my wife and I never make plans for how we can take the next step, neither do we come up with any strategies of our own. The plans we receive always come through encounters with Jesus Christ. Lately, we have been led to take some major new steps into unknown territory, as the Father has led us in new ways to fulfill the vision that He has given to us. These new steps have been a direct consequence of us seeing new sides of the love of the Father. This has given us restful and peaceful increase.

Renewing the Mind

Revelation reforms our heart and as a result, we are transformed. As our hearts are reformed by revelation, we are transformed by the renewing of our minds: *"And do not be conformed to this world, but be transformed by the renewing of your mind, so that you may prove what the will of God is, that which is good and acceptable and perfect"* (Rom. 12:2 NASB). A renewed mind has started to align itself with the ways and purposes of God, which is how we can begin to partner with His plan for our lives. The renewing of the mind happens, as we keep drinking from the revelation that God has provided. This is the reason why it is important for us to be good stewards of revelation and be quick to respond to His call.

Partnering with God-given Revelation

We have seen how Paul was forever changed by his encounter with the risen Christ. The encounter that Paul had with Jesus on the road to Damascus are recounted three times, within the book of Acts. The last record of Paul sharing his experiences with the risen Jesus takes place as he is being questioned by king Agrippa. He tells the king how he responded to this revelation that came directly from Jesus Christ Himself:

"For that reason, King Agrippa, I did not prove disobedient to the heavenly vision, but continually proclaimed to those in Damascus first and in Jerusalem and then all the region of Judea and even to the

Gentiles, that they are to repent and turn to God, performing deeds consistent with repentance" (Acts 26:19-20 NASB).

Paul was not disobedient to the revelation he had received from Jesus. Paul partnered with the love of Jesus Christ, by preaching the gospel to the gentiles. When we receive more revelation from the Father, it transforms us so that we can reflect Jesus more. As we partner with the will of God, we are empowered to break out of old religious boxes and traditions to take new territories and spheres for God. Our responsibility is to have a heart that is open to receive from the Father and to be willing to obey what we see.

Activations

- The life of the apostle Paul was reshaped by revelation from God. How has revelation transformed your life? Take some time to reflect on this. Write down the fruit of revelation that you have seen in your own life.

- Take 20-30 minutes in prayer. Ask the Holy Spirit to give more revelation to you in the three specific areas mentioned here. Ask Him to illuminate your heart in these areas:

  1. *The heart of the Father and the finished work of Jesus Christ.*
  2. *Your inheritance as a child of God.*
  3. *The calling and purpose that you have in Christ.*

  Write down what he shows you in these three areas.

- Revelation reforms our heart. Ask the Holy Spirit to reveal areas in your heart that need to be reformed. Ask Him to illuminate these areas with revelation and give Him permission to reform your inner life. Write down the areas He shows you, as well as the insights you receive.

- Take 20-30 minutes in prayer. Ask the Father to pour out revelation on the body of Christ, so that we receive fresh manna from heaven. Does He show you specific areas where we need to grow in revelation? If so, write down what He reveals and keep praying for the body of Christ.

CHAPTER 2: REVELATION AND SONSHIP

As our revelation of the Father grows deeper, we will gain more insight into who we are in Christ as well. If you have been called to birth and build a vision from God, you need to be established in your identity and sonship. One important principle within the Kingdom of God is that whatever we do for God is always meant to flow out of who we are. To operate from our identity in Christ, we need to know that we are our Father's beloved kids. Since our identity describes our position as His children, we can't embrace our identity without knowing the Father's heart. Our identity is always revealed as we abide in His love.

I have learned to define myself as my Father's radically favored and beloved son. I do a lot of things in the Kingdom of God, such as writing books, teaching in seminars and preaching, but that's not where I find my identity as a believer. My identity is found in Christ alone. It has been extremely liberating to know that I can have all my security and confidence in Christ. Knowing that I am my Father's beloved son has set me free from the pressure of falling into a performance-based model of ministry. It has also kept me from the temptation of finding my identity in the results and blessings of our work.

The Father Lavishes His Love Upon Us

Look with wonder at the depth of the Father's marvelous love that he has lavished on us! He has called us and made us his very own beloved children. The reason the world doesn't recognize who we are is that they didn't recognize him (1 John 3:1 The Passion).

When the Bible describes the Father's love towards His children, it doesn't use a balanced language. It always uses a language of overflow by speaking of lavishing and abundant love. The Father loves us more than we could even begin to understand. We are the apple of His eyes, who delight His heart in a deep way. He has lavished all His marvelous love upon us and He calls us His own children. He does all this because He wants us as His own. We did not choose Him, but He invited us into His own family. For those of us who have been rejected and abandoned by one or both of our parents, this is very good news. We find true healing in knowing that long before any earthly parent had ever rejected us, our heavenly Father had already chosen us as His own child. The orphan identity is a big lie. The truth is that we have always had the best Father in the world. He has always longed to bring us home to Himself. Abiding in the love of the Father transforms us into generous and creative people that are set ablaze with a holy fire from heaven.

The World Does Not Recognize Us

Since the world does not know the Father, it can't recognize who we are. Because of this, we need to be careful when it comes to whom we're allowing to define and influence us. It is important that we learn to live according to our identity as children of God, because only He sees us as we truly are. If we look to the world to gain a better self-image, we might find some good help and a few good tools for that. But the help we might receive will still be very limited, because the world doesn't know our identity in Christ. We need the Holy Spirit to know who we are. If we don't know the heart of the Father and His love for us, we will still be orphans, no matter how much we work with our self-image. We might be orphans with a little bit better self-esteem, but only the love of the Father can provide true sonship.

The Lie of the Orphan Identity

The orphan identity has its origin in Satan. He is the first orphan and he chose the orphan lifestyle by rebelling against God's rule.

As a result of his rebellion, Satan lost everything and was thrown down into the grave (Isa. 14:12-16). His ultimate goal is to deceive us to embrace an orphan identity, so that we end up being bound in the same misery as he is. Satan wants us to lose our identity and inheritance just like he did. He tries to make that happen by deceiving us into believing that the Father is not interested in us. He wants us to believe that we are not worthy to be loved.

If we listen to these lies, we will be tricked into living as orphans, even though we're already abiding in the Father's house all the time. The orphan is someone who has lost his parents and as a result, has no home, no roots, no inheritance. Because of this, the life of an orphan will become a lifestyle of constant struggle for identity, belonging and inheritance (See *Abiding in the Father's Love,* for an in-depth study of the orphan identity).

We need to realize that the orphan identity is based on a lie. As a child of God, you are not an orphan anymore. You're a beloved son or daughter and the Father's heart towards you, is for you to know that you are His chosen and beloved child. Jesus declared to us that *"I will not leave you as orphans; I am coming to you" (John 14:18 NASB).* This statement reveals what Jesus accomplished for us through the cross. We are not orphans anymore. We live in the presence of the Father all the time and as we keep abiding in His love and approval, we will learn to live out of our identity in Christ. We are now co-heirs with Jesus Christ and have received our glorious inheritance with every heavenly blessing in Christ.

Only the Father Can Provide Sonship

As we have seen, we find our identity in Christ by knowing the heart of the Father. The reason for this is that only the Father can provide real identity to a son. Being a son is not about gender in this context, but here it speaks of a spiritual position. Both men and women receive the full inheritance of sonship, when they receive Jesus. *"Because you are sons, God has sent forth the Spirit of*

His Son into our hearts, crying, "Abba! Father!" Therefore you are no longer a slave, but a son; and if a son, then an heir through God" (Gal. 4:6-7 NASB). Every time the Bible makes a statement concerning who we are in Christ, it describes an aspect of the inheritance that we have received as sons. The Father's love shapes our lives, so we can live out of our identity in Christ and receive His promises. This doesn't happen all at once. It is a lifelong process of learning to abide in His love and discover more of who we are in Christ. When we allow that process to happen, His love brings healing to our heart and soul. Rejection and abandonment will no longer find a place in our heart. Instead, we will be filled by the loving acceptance of the Father, so that we can live in a close fellowship with Jesus Christ, who promised to never leave nor forsake us.

We Were Chosen by the Father

We have already seen that it was the Father who chose us and not the other way around. This truth is foundational for knowing that we are accepted by God. Paul writes on this topic in his letter to the Ephesians:

And in love he chose us before he laid the foundation of the universe! Because of his great love, he ordained us, so that we would be seen as holy in his eyes with an unstained innocence. For it was always in his perfect plan to adopt us as his delightful children, through our union with Jesus, the Anointed One, so that his tremendous love that cascades over us would glorify his grace —for the same love he has for the Beloved, Jesus, he has for us. And this unfolding plan brings him great pleasure (Eph. 1:4-6 The Passion)!

To realize that we were chosen by the Father, even before He laid the foundation of the world is mind-blowing. The creator of the universe looked through time and space and saw us. He liked us so much that He chose us to become His children. The Father has always been longing to reveal Himself to us and invite us to be part of His family.

We need to realize that He wants us in His presence. He loves us so much that Jesus went through death and resurrection to bring us home to the Father. The Father loves us in the same way that He loves His Son. I have ministered to so many people through the years, who expressed a belief that they were a mistake and that they were unworthy to be loved. But no one has ever been unwanted or a mistake. The Father has chosen you and He wants to lavish His love upon you. When you allow the Holy Spirit to minister to your heart, His approval and love will bring healing to the broken places in your soul. He will continue His work until you realize and embrace that you are a chosen and beloved child of God.

My Process of Embracing Sonship

When I look back at my own journey of learning to live as a son, it didn't happen all at once. The Father brought me through the process of being delivered and healed from my orphan identity. This process took a couple of years, but during this time He did a thorough work within my heart. When my heart was healed by His love, a new foundation was laid in my life. I now know that I am His beloved and favored son and heir. This has become my foundation and my identity. This is not true only about me, but every believer is His beloved, favored and blessed child!

The Transforming Power of His Love

We read from 1 John 3:1 earlier in this chapter, but let's continue by reading the next verse: *"Beloved, we are God's children right now; however, it is not yet apparent what we will become. But we do know that when it is finally made visible, we will be just like him, for we will see him as he truly is"* (1 John 3:2 The Passion). We are His children now, but at the same time we are becoming something new. At times, it will be hard for us to understand the transforming work of the Holy Spirit within our lives. But we can trust that the goal of all transformation will be Christlikeness. The Holy Spirit will always work toward that end. This is our sure foundation. *"And this hope is not a disappointing fantasy, because we can now experience the endless love of God cascading into our hearts through the Holy Spirit who lives in us"* (Rom. 5:5 *The Passion*)! Our lives are meant to mirror the life of Jesus Christ. Jesus was sent to this world to reveal the heart of the Father and that is our calling as well. Jesus was sent to heal the brokenhearted and to proclaim freedom for the captives and we are sent to do likewise. A life of true sonship always mirrors the life Jesus.

Activations

- The Father lavishes His love upon you in abundance. Take 20-30 minutes in prayer, where you ask Him to shower you with His love. Then quiet yourself before Him and drink in His love.

- We saw how the journey from the orphan identity to sonship is a process. Where are you in this process? Are there areas in your life where you still struggle with the orphan identity? Take some time to reflect on this and write down any insights you receive. Ask the Father to pour His love into areas of your heart, where you need to be healed from the orphan wound.

- We read from 1 John 3:1-2 in this chapter. Spend some time with the Holy Spirit and reflect on these verses together with Him. Ask Him to illuminate your heart and give more revelation on this passage. Write down what He reveals to you.

- Spend some time interceding for the body of Christ. Ask for a deeper revelation of sonship and identity in Christ to come upon us and for us to receive wisdom to steward this revelation in a good way.

CHAPTER 3: OUR RIGHTS AS SONS

But when the time of fulfillment had come, God sent his Son, born of a woman, born under the law. Yet all of this was so that he would redeem and set free those held hostage to the law so that we would receive our freedom and a full legal adoption as his children (Gal. 4:4-5 TPT).

A very empowering aspect of living as sons and daughters in the kingdom of God is that we now have received the full rights to our inheritance in Christ. Knowing this truth is foundational for us if we want to live a victorious life. It will help us when we aim to take new ground for the Kingdom of God. We have been made heirs and ambassadors for Jesus Christ, which means that our Father has given us His full permission and mandate to represent Him right here and now. We are anointed and equipped to rule and reign together with Jesus in this world (Rom. 5:17).

The word adoption mentioned in the text above, doesn't have the meaning that we might think as westerners. This doesn't refer to parents adopting a child that is not their own. Rather, it refers to parents adopting their own child into the family. Let me explain a little more. The Greek word translated as adoption here, is the word *"huiothesia"*, which literally means *"the placing as a son, i.e. adoption" (Strong's p. 1678).* This word speaks of a son taking his place as an adult son. It was used as a reference to a ceremony in which a minor son was initiated into full family status, by being given the full rights and privileges of an adult son. It symbolized maturity, the bestowing of the full rights of sonship upon the son who already belonged to the family. This is what our Father has done for us through Jesus Christ.

The Law Was Our Guardian

We read that Jesus delivered us from the law, so that we could receive our full inheritance as sons and daughters. He did that by liberating us from the law. Up until that time humanity had been in bondage to it and it operated as our guardian. Even the gentiles have the law written in their conscience, which is why it is called the elemental spiritual force of this world. Legalism and religion can be found in every culture, even if it's not expressed specifically as the ten commandments.

What I am saying is that as long as an heir is underage, he is no different from a slave, although he owns the whole estate. The heir is subject to guardians and trustees until the time set by his father. So also, when we were underage, we were in slavery under the elemental spiritual forces of the world (Gal. 4:1-3 NIV).

This is a general truth about how we were slaves under the law before we got saved, but this is true for us on an individual level as well. If we have not yet experienced the freedom of the New Covenant, we are still operating under the heavy burden of the law, which makes it impossible for us to receive the full benefits of our rights as children of God. We will then be conditioned to live in spiritual slavery again, even though our full inheritance is available to us in Christ. Legalism conditions us to live for God's approval. It creates a lifestyle where we try to earn His blessings. That way of relating to the Father has no place in sonship and it hinders us from experiencing the full blessing of our inheritance.

The good news is that God's intention is for us to be delivered from all legalism, so that we can live in the full freedom that Jesus has provided through His finished work on the cross. Our Father always completes the work that He has started within us. We can be confident that His plan to set us free will work (Phil. 1:6). If we allow Him to shape our lives, we will be delivered from all religious striving and exchange the yoke of legalism and religion for the glorious lifestyle of abiding in our Father's love.

Being Filled with the Spirit of Sonship

In a moment, we will define what it looks like to fully receive our rights as sons and to live in the freedom that we have in Christ, but first we need to look at how the Holy Spirit works to establish us in sonship. The Spirit is our wonderful Helper and we surely need all the help we can get, because we can neither grasp, nor receive our new identity by ourselves. *"Because you are his sons, God sent the Spirit of his Son into our hearts, the Spirit who calls out, "Abba, Father." So you are no longer a slave, but God's child; and since you are his child, God has made you also an heir"* (Gal. 4:6-7 NIV). The Father has sent the Holy Spirit into our hearts to call out *"Abba Father"* from within our hearts, until this cry becomes the prayer of our hearts as well. This is how we'll find deliverance from the spiritual slavery of being under the law.

As the Holy Spirit helps us in this way, we will grow into our full identity as heirs of God and we can then start to live as mature sons and daughters that represent the heart of our loving Father well. Paul explains this same truth, in His letter to the Romans: *"And by him we cry, 'Abba, Father.' The Spirit himself testifies with our spirit that we are God's children. Now if we are children, then we are heirs—heirs of God and co-heirs with Christ, if indeed we share in his sufferings in order that we may also share in his glory"* (Rom. 8:15-16 NIV). Being mature children of God means that we live out of our inheritance in Christ, ruling and reigning with Him, so that the heart of the Father is revealed through our lifestyle.

Jesus Stepped into His Inheritance as the Firstborn Son

Jesus experienced the ceremony of son-placing where the Father granted Him the full rights as the firstborn Son by the baptism in the Jordan river. From that moment He began to operate in His full inheritance as the Christ, the anointed One. The Holy Spirit descended like a dove upon Jesus and anointed Him with power. As that was happening, the Father made a powerful declaration over His beloved Son, by expressing His deep love for Him:

When He had been baptized, Jesus came up immediately from the water; and behold, the heavens were opened to Him and He saw the Spirit of God descending like a dove and alighting upon Him. And suddenly a voice came from heaven, saying, "This is My beloved Son, in whom I am well pleased (Matt. 3:16-17 NKJV).

Jesus entered His ministry as the Christ at that moment. His first mission was to overcome all the devil's temptations in the desert. He then started to preach the gospel of the Kingdom with signs and wonders following. Jesus was operating in the full authority of sonship and He walked in extreme favor, with both God and man. This had never happened before. Luke describes how the ministry of Jesus impacted Galilee: *"And Jesus returned to Galilee in the power of the Spirit and news about Him spread through all the surrounding region. And He began teaching in their synagogues and was praised by all"* (Luke 4:14-15 NASB). Jesus was moving in His inheritance as the firstborn Son. By doing that, He shows us the power and authority of sonship. For the first time in history, the world could witness a man who fully operated in his rights and authority as a son of God. Through the life of Jesus, the Father has given a perfect example of what a lifestyle of abiding in His love looks like.

Every son and daughter of God can now operate in that same anointing and favor that rested upon Jesus. This has always been the Father's plan. *"For those whom He foreknew, He also predestined to become conformed to the image of His Son, so that He would be the firstborn among many brothers and sisters"* (Rom. 8:29 NASB). Jesus was commissioned to reveal the heart of the Father to the world, but He also sent us to do the same. This is very good news for us!

The Anointing of the Firstborn Son

When Jesus returned to His hometown Nazareth, He entered the synagogue. While He was attending the service there, He read a portion of scripture from the book of Isaiah: *"The Spirit of the Lord is upon Me, because He anointed Me to bring good news to the poor. He has sent Me to proclaim release to captives and recovery of sight to the blind, to set free those who are oppressed, to proclaim the favorable year of the Lord" (Luke 4:18-19 NASB).* This prophetic declaration reveals the anointing that were to rest upon the Messiah and it describes what it looks like, when the Son operates in His rights and inheritance. Jesus continues: *"And He rolled up the scroll, gave it back to the attendant and sat down; and the eyes of all the people in the synagogue were intently directed at Him. Now He began to say to them, 'Today this Scripture has been fulfilled in your hearing'" (Luke 4:20-21 NASB).* This Scripture was being fulfilled right in front of them, as the firstborn Son of God was ministering in their midst. This passage has been called the Messiah's mandate, which it is. But it also describes the mandate of mature children of God, who represent the Father by operating in their full inheritance. When we tap into all the blessings and rights of our sonship, we will be able to walk in the same power as Jesus did. Creation itself longs for the full manifestation of the children of God to be revealed in the earth (Rom. 8:19).

As He Is, So Are We in This World

When we were born again, we were placed as sons, which means that we have the same standing with our Father as Jesus Himself. *"Herein is our love made perfect, that we may have boldness in the day of judgment: because as he is, so are we in this world" (1 John 4:17).* Since we are now in Christ, we will find our true identity by knowing who He is. Our identity is revealed in Him. Jesus is the firstborn among many brethren and we look just like Him. The life and ministry of Jesus is the blueprint for our life and ministry as well. We have received our Father's full approval and we have been anointed with the Holy Spirit. We have access to our full rights and inheritance as mature sons of God. We are called to represent our Father and we have been sent to reveal Jesus in this world. We now have access to the same anointing and favor that Jesus operated in. Our Father believes in us and He expects us to represent Him well.

What It Looks Like to Operate in Our Rights as Sons

While Peter preached the gospel of the Kingdom at Cornelius' house, he described the ministry of Christ in the following way: *"You know of Jesus of Nazareth, how God anointed Him with the Holy Spirit and with power and how He went about doing good and healing all who were oppressed by the devil, for God was with Him"* (Acts 10:38 *NASB*). Since our lives are meant to reflect the life of Christ, this text describes what the ministry of the children of God looks like. It will be said of us that we are the sons and daughters who *"went about doing good and healing all who were oppressed by the devil"*.

As we have already seen, Luke 4:18-19 describes the anointing that rests upon the sons and daughters of God. That passage is our job description. It reveals five important things that we have been anointed to accomplish. But before I list these, I want us to read from Isaiah 61, where we'll find this famous prophecy about the Messiah's mandate that Jesus quoted in Nazareth. When we continue to read where Jesus stopped in Luke 4, we'll find some more points that we can add to our job description.

… to proclaim the year of the Lord's favor and the day of vengeance of our God, to comfort all who mourn and provide for those who grieve in Zion— to bestow on them a crown of beauty instead of ashes, the oil of joy instead of mourning and a garment of praise instead of a spirit of despair (Isa. 61:2-3 *NIV*).

When we combine Luke 4 and Isaiah 61, we'll find the following list of things that we have been anointed to do as children of God:

- *The Spirit of the Lord is upon Me, because He anointed Me to bring good news to the poor.*
  We have been anointed and sent to preach the gospel to a world that is longing for some good news about Jesus. Every human being who doesn't know Jesus is in a state of spiritual poverty and it is our privilege to introduce them to the unsearchable riches of Christ.

- *He has sent Me to proclaim release to captives.*
  There is a lot of captivity in our world today. People are bound by all kinds of sins and destructive habits. Many even live in captivity without knowing it. We have been sent to break these bondages, so that these captives can go free (Isa. 58:6).

- *Recovery of sight to the blind.*
  Jesus will open the blind eyes through us. This statement applies to both physical and spiritual blindness. When we're representing and revealing the heart of the Father to the world, the people we minister to will recover their spiritual sight and get to know God as He really is.

- *To set free those who are oppressed.*
  We read how Jesus healed all who have been oppressed by the devil. This is our calling as sons and daughters as well. Wherever we discern demonic oppression binding people, we have authority to set them free.

- *To proclaim the favorable year of the Lord.*
  We're living in the year of the favor of the Lord and this is the day of salvation (2 Cor. 6:1-2). It's now our time to proclaim the good news of the gospel. We are living in a day when Jesus wants to reveal His unmerited favor to the world through us. We have been anointed to preach the good news of the gospel.

- ***Proclaiming the day of vengeance of our God.***
  This does not refer to the vengeance of the Lord upon us, but it speaks about destroying the works of the devil. We have been anointed to break demonic activity and bring full restoration and recompense from the damage that he has caused (1 John 3:8).

- ***To comfort all who mourn.***
  Our God is the Father of mercy and God of all comfort. We reveal His heart by comforting those who mourn. As we show mercy by comforting the broken, many will be made whole again by the loving embrace of heaven.

- ***Bestow on them a crown of beauty instead of ashes.***
  Wounds, failures and brokenness sometimes look like a pile of ashes. A lot of people believe that this is who they are, but that is not their true identity. The Father wants them to know that they are His beloved children and He wants to crown them with beauty and favor through our ministry of healing and restoration.

- ***Bestowing the oil of gladness instead of mourning.***
  The joy of the Lord is our strength and to rejoice in the Holy Spirit is foundational to a child of God. Our Father wants to anoint the broken with the oil of gladness. This is what we have been sent to do, comforting the one who mourns and to release the oil of joy.

- ***Bestowing a garment of praise instead of a disheartened spirit.*** The Father wants us to live a lifestyle of praise and worship. That is the best medicine for hopelessness and discouragement. The Father has sent us into the world to break every yoke of discouragement and bestow the garments of praise.

As we embrace our inheritance as children of God, the world will be transformed. The ministry of sonship will look like Isaiah 61 and Luke 4:17-18. In other words, we're going to operate in the Messiah's mandate. You should boldly expect this anointing to manifest through your life as you embrace your sonship. We tap into the anointing of sonship by abiding in the Father's love. This transforms us into becoming the peculiar people that is called the manifested sons of God.

The Father Wants to Minister to Us

We need to hear our Father speak love and approval to us every day. As Jesus is, so are we in this world. The same declaration of love, approval and pleasure that the Father spoke over Jesus, He is now speaking into our heart, as well. We need to hear these words everyday: *You are my beloved child and I'm well pleased with you.* I have asked my Father to speak these words into my heart every day. His words both comforts, encourage and restore my soul. Knowing that my Father is well pleased with me has been one of the most profound revelations in my life. As you keep on drinking from His love, all the blessings that are listed above will manifest in your life as well. You will receive a crown of beauty and wear the garments of praise. You will walk in healing and increasing joy. You will become freer and experience a greater favor because your Father loves you!

Activations

- You have received the full rights of sonship. This means that you have the authority to represent your heavenly Father. Take some time to reflect on this truth. Invite the Holy Spirit to show you how this affects your life. Write down any insight you will get.

- The same words of love that the Father spoke over Jesus, He wants to speak into your heart: *You are my beloved child and I'm well pleased with you.* Spend some time in prayer and listen to the Father, as He speaks these words of love and approval into your heart. Write down the words He speaks to you.

- In this chapter, we looked at the anointing of sonship, as described in Luke 4 and Isaiah 61. Go back and read the list that describes what we have been anointed to do as children of God. Which manifestations of the anointing mentioned there do you already operate in? Do you long to see some of them manifest more? Ask the Holy Spirit to reveal more on this topic to you. Write down what He reveals to you.

- Take 20-30 minutes to pray through the list from Luke 4 and Isaiah 61. Jesus wants you to have these blessings in your life, but He also wants to release them through you into this world. Ask the Father to release these blessings in your personal life. Ask him to anoint you to minister in the anointing of sonship, so that the heart of the Father can be revealed to the world through you.

CHAPTER 4: SONSHIP AND NEW CREATION REALITIES

We are sons and daughters of God and we have received our full inheritance in Christ. This phrase, *in Christ,* is very important to keep in mind, when studying our identity as children of God. In fact, every time that the Bible reveals some aspect of who we are in Christ, it describes our identity as our Father's children. When we understand this, we realize that one of the main themes of the Bible is sonship. Jesus came to restore us into sonship, with all its blessings and benefits. In this chapter, we're going to look at who we are in Christ to dig out even more revelation on our identity as sons and daughters of God. By being in Christ, we are a new creation, which is why I like to call the biblical truths that reveal who we are in Christ, new creation realities.

The New Birth

When we got saved, we were born again and filled with the life of God. Paul speaks about the new birth in these famous words: *"Therefore, if anyone is in Christ, he is a new creation; old things have passed away; behold, all things have become new"* (2 Cor. 5:17 NKJV). Being born again is to be placed in Christ and to become a brand-new creation. Through Christ, we have been delivered from the old, fallen identity of the flesh and received a new identity. This new identity is only found in Christ. When we see who we are in Him, we can start to live from our identity as sons and daughters in a much deeper way. This is son-placing in action!

There are two different streams in the body of Christ that have had a strong influence on me. One of these streams focuses a lot on our identity in Christ and faith. The other stream focuses on the heart of the Father and a revelation of His love. These streams have developed very different cultures and they use a somewhat different terminology. Because of this, I had the impression that I needed to choose which of these streams I wanted to be part of, but no such choice was needed, since these truths are two sides of the same coin. My identity in Christ defines my sonship and it holds the key for me to live in my full inheritance. But the key to live in my identity in Christ is to abide in the Father's love and know His heart. I can only be established in my identity as a son by knowing my Father. Trying to live out of my identity in Christ with the heart of an orphan easily becomes legalism.

I also realized that to be secure in my sonship and to enjoy all its benefits, I needed to know my identity in Christ. My identity in Christ defines both my sonship and inheritance. I saw how many people tried to live in their sonship without really knowing their identity in Christ. These people often ended up being stuck, since all they had to hold on to, was their emotional experiences. They were always seeking a new experience of the love of the Father, but that became a kind of legalism as well. This left people stuck in the pattern of always seeking experiences, but never entering their rest in Christ. I am grateful that I knew my identity in Christ when I received a deeper revelation of the Father. That created a place for His love to land within my soul. I found rest in knowing that I am His beloved, blessed and perfect son! Throughout the rest of this chapter, we are going to study our identity as children of God, by discovering who we are in Christ.

New Creation Realities

I have already mentioned that all new creation realities reveal different aspects of our identity as the Father's children. It is very empowering to live in intimacy with the Father, knowing that we are part of His royal and holy family. We are now the manifested children of God that all of creation has been longing to see. Being a new creation comes with so many blessings, that many books could be written to describe even a fragment of the unsearchable riches we have received in Christ. Now, I want to share some of the new creation realities that specifically benefit us in living out our calling and building the vision God has given to us.

You Are a Righteous Child

To be righteous means being justified and declared innocent by God. Jesus accomplished our righteousness through His work on the cross: *"For He made Him who knew no sin to be sin for us, that we might become the righteousness of God in Him" (2 Cor. 5:21 NKJV).* Jesus became sin for us to make us into the righteousness of God in Him. He became as we are, so that we could become as He is. Through the finished work of Christ, all guilt has been removed and our innocence has been fully restored. It is as if we had never committed any sins at all, in the Father's eyes. Our dignity has been restored. Because of this, we are now totally righteous sons and daughters of God. Knowing that we have been justified by grace alone gives us confidence in our life with Jesus. We never need to wonder if our mistakes could cause us to fall out of favor with God. There is no stain on us anymore and Jesus has carried our sins away, which makes us His righteous children!

You Are a Holy and Perfect Child

Through the cross of Christ, we have been totally sanctified and perfected forever. *"By that will we have been sanctified through the offering of the body of Jesus Christ once for all… For by one offering He has perfected forever those who are being sanctified" (Hebr. 10:10, 14 NKJV).* On the cross, Jesus became one with our incompleteness and uncleannessto make us fully complete and clean in Christ. Because of this, we are now sanctified and perfected forever. This gives us great boldness. There is no need for us to wonder what the Father might think of us anymore. This sets us free to walk with Him in bold assurance and confidence. When the Father looks at us, He sees perfection and completeness!

You Are Dead to Sin

Not only have we been set free from the guilt and stain of all our past sins. We have been delivered from the power of sin as well. *"Likewise reckon ye also yourselves to be dead indeed unto sin, but alive unto God through Jesus Christ our Lord" (Rom. 6:11).* Jesus not only died for us, but He died as us. Since we were crucified and died with Him, we have died to sin. Sin has neither power, nor a claim on us anymore. Through the cross of Christ, we have been fully delivered from both the power and consequences of sin. We have no reason to fear the power of sin. I meet many believers who are afraid to fall into sin while in ministry, mainly because they have heard or read about fallen leaders and pioneers from the history of the church. These leaders ended up hurting a lot of people and created a lot of damage through their failures. We need to walk in humility to bear lasting fruit, but we shouldn't walk in fear of the power of sin. We are dead to sin, so that we can live fully for our Lord Jesus Christ (Rom. 6:1-11)!

You Are Alive and Have Life in Abundance

Not only have we died with Christ, but we have been made alive in Him as well. The Father has filled us with an abundance of His very own life. *"A thief has only one thing in mind —he wants to steal, slaughter and destroy. But I have come to give you everything in abundance, more than you expect —life in its fullness until you overflow" (John 10:10 TPT).* When we minister to people, we bring life that overflows. Our dreams and visions will release the life of God, so that the body of Christ is revived and renewed! This is who we are. We bring life, renewal and revival wherever we go, because of the life of God overflowing through us!

You Are Healed and Whole

Through the wounds of Jesus Christ, we have been made whole and He is our shepherd who brings us into full restoration. *"Our instant healing flowed from his wounding. You were like sheep that continually wandered away, but now you have returned to the true Shepherd of your lives—the kind Guardian who lovingly watches over your souls"* (1 Pet. 2:24-25 TPT). Jesus became one with our pain, wounds and brokenness to make us whole. Since it's sometimes can be painful to serve God and to walk out a vision, this is good news for us. Broken and hurt people will hurt people and every vision from God will attract broken people. Spiritual attacks and persecution are painful as well, but through it all, there is a river of healing flowing from heaven that flows from His scars to make us whole again (Isa. 53:3-5).

You Are a Royal Priesthood

We are our Father's royal and priestly children. *"Now to the one who constantly loves us and has loosed us from our sins by his own blood and to the one who has appointed us as a kingdom of priests to serve his God and Father—to him be glory and dominion throughout the eternity of eternities! Amen"* (Rev. 1:5-6 TPT). Jesus Himself has redeemed us, both from sins and a fallen identity. He has made us a royal priesthood. As His kings, we are His ambassadors in the world, representing Him by releasing His Kingdom. As His priests, we represent the world in the heavenly realm by carrying the nations and people before the Father in prayer. Being part of a royal family is to be born into dignity and nobility. As our Father's royal and priestly children, we build our vision with dignity and nobility, so that the world can be transformed by the love of the Father!

Jesus broke the bondages of religion, sin and Satan on the cross to make us free. *"Stand fast therefore in the liberty wherewith Christ hath made us free and be not entangled again with the yoke of bondage"* *(Gal. 5:21).* We have been set free to live the life that Jesus wants us to live. He wants us to live in the joy, peace and righteousness of the Holy Spirit, being fully rooted and grounded in His love. As we walk out our vision together with Jesus, we are free from everything that tries to bind us. We are not bound or defined by religion and we can't be placed in religious boxes anymore. We have been delivered into a life of freedom in Christ. Our dreams and visions will reveal the freedom that is found in Christ, so that the people we are called to serve will find deliverance from all kinds of oppression. This includes being set free from the power of sin, demonic bondages and the oppression of religion.

You Are Fruitful

Jesus broke all barrenness on the cross to make us fruitful. *"You did not choose me, but I chose you and appointed you so that you might go and bear fruit—fruit that will last—and so that whatever you ask in my name the Father will give you"* *(John 15:16 NIV).* Many believers have been trapped in a cycle of lack and have not seen the results they expected, but Jesus broke this cycle on the cross. Because of this, being fruitful is our identity. As we build our vision and live our God-given dreams, we can expect lasting fruit. We will also raise up fruitful people through our lives and ministries. This is our birthright as children of God!

You Are Blessed

Jesus became a curse for us, so that we could receive the fullness of the Father's heavenly blessings. *"All praise to God, the Father of our Lord Jesus Christ, who has blessed us with every spiritual blessing in the heavenly realms because we are united with Christ" (Eph. 1:3 NLT).* We have received every blessing that heaven has to offer. When we walk into a room, a service, or into our workplace, we bring the full blessing of the Father. We are His blessed children and we can expect our vision and ministry to be blessed and for the favor of God to rest upon all that we do. Our ministry will set people free from a cursed life by releasing the blessing of heaven. We are blessed to be a blessing (1 Pet. 3:8-9).

You Are a Lover

Jesus overcame all hate and bitterness on the cross, so that the love of the Father could be poured into the hearts of His children. *"Now hope does not disappoint, because the love of God has been poured out in our hearts by the Holy Spirit who was given to us" (Rom. 5:5 NKJV).* The love of the Father has been poured into our hearts. It is now natural for us to love both God and people. Bitterness and hate are not compatible with our new identity, which is why it is a torment to have it in our lives. Because we have His love in our hearts, we have the strength to build our vision according to His heart, constantly growing in love. We love because He first loved us (1 John 4:19).

You Are More than a Conqueror

Jesus overcame the devil on the cross and stripped the demonic realm of its weapons. Because of this, we have already won the spiritual battle. *"Yet in all these things we are more than conquerors through Him who loved us" (Rom. 8:37 NKJV).* We have been born again to overcome and conquer in the spiritual battle. This is not something that we have to do by our own efforts. This is who we are. If we are rooted in Christ, overcoming will come as a fruit of that. We conquer new territory for the Kingdom of God and raise up more overcomers for Christ, simply because this is who we are created to be!

The Power of Living from Our Identity in Christ

As believers, we are meant to live *from* our identity in Christ, but I have noticed that many believers live *for* identity instead. The new creation realities listed above, illustrate the amazing power of knowing our identity in Christ when we walk out our calling. In Christ, we have received everything we need to do whatever God calls us to do. Everything that we do in the Kingdom of God is meant to flow out of our identity in Christ and a revelation of the heart of the Father. We will find the freedom, boldness and wisdom to live in Christ by abiding in our Father's love!

- Sonship and our identity in Christ are two sides of the same coin. Reflect on this truth for a while. How does knowing who you are in Christ, bring you deeper into the heart of the Father? How does abiding in the love of the Father help you to live in Christ? Invite the Holy Spirit to give you more insight on this topic. Write down any revelation that you might receive.

- Read the list of new creation realities in this chapter. Ask the Holy Spirit to highlight the truths about your identity that you need to be more established in. Take some time in prayer and ask Jesus to strengthen your foundation and bring healing to you in these areas.

- Spend 20-30 minutes in prayer. Ask Jesus to complete the list of new creation realities in this chapter for you. Invite Him to reveal more truths about your identity in Christ. Write down what He reveals to you and ask Him to take you deeper into these realities.

- Take some time to pray and intercede for the body of Christ. Ask the Father to bring a deeper revelation on the love of the Father and our identity in Christ to us. Ask Him to bring us into deeper encounters with His heart.

CHAPTER 5: THE FIVEFOLD DNA OF JESUS IN AND THROUGH US

It is important for us to understand that every believer has been ordained and anointed as a minister of the New Covenant. This means that we are called to have Christlike influence, both on the body of Christ and in the world. For that to happen, we must be conformed into the image of Jesus Christ, so that our lives reflect His. The Father's ultimate goal is to conform all His children into the image of Christ. It is important that we don't assume that this means us becoming nameless and faceless clones:

But that doesn't mean you should all look and speak and act the same. Out of the generosity of Christ, each of us is given his own gift. The text for this is, He climbed the high mountain, He captured the enemy and seized the plunder, He handed it all out in gifts to the people (Eph. 4:7-8, The Message).

The more we are being conformed into the image of His Son, we will also be restored into the original person that the Father has created us to be. It takes the whole body of Christ to reveal the fullness of Jesus to the world. This can only happen because Jesus lives in us and reveals His life through us.

The Life of Jesus Christ

The essence of ministry in the New Covenant is to allow Jesus to express His life through us. The big difference between ministry under the law, compared to ministry under grace is that religion will tell us to live *for* Jesus. The gospel reveals that we have been crucified with Christ and that He now lives His life *through* us:

"I have been crucified with Christ and I no longer live, but Christ lives in me. The life I now live in the body, I live by faith in the Son of God, who loved me and gave himself for me" (Gal. 2:20 NIV).

We have already been crucified with Christ. He is our source of life now and we have died, so that Jesus can live through us. All our gifts and the anointing of the Holy Spirit are expressions of the life of Jesus flowing through us. They simply reflect different aspects of Christ.

Jesus Can Be Whatever He Wants to Be Through Us

The revelation that unlocks a New Covenant lifestyle is that Jesus lives in us and wants to express His life through us. *"To them God has chosen to make known among the Gentiles the glorious riches of this mystery, which is Christ in you, the hope of glory" (Col. 1:27 NIV).* Knowing that we have died so that Jesus can live through us is foundational for our ministry as well. This revelation will affect every area of our life with God. It changes our understanding of ministry in a powerful way. One of the most frequently asked questions is how I found my calling and purpose in life. I always answer that the main purpose of my life is to make room for Jesus to be whatever He wants to be in and through me. Every calling in the Kingdom of God is always about allowing Jesus to express Himself through us. He charges our gifts with His own life and empowers us with His grace, so that we can live out our purpose. The ministry gifts are perfect examples of this reality. These gifts are all expressions of Jesus Himself. New Covenant ministry will always come down to allowing Jesus to express His life through us. Our job is to surrender and give Him room to work through us. This is grace in action!

Jesus Is the Ministry Gifts

Because the fivefold ministry represents different aspects of the ministry of Jesus, the DNA of these ministries are present within every believer. We can tap into it whenever we need to do so. For example, every believer will probably not become an apostle, but every believer carries apostolic DNA and can therefore move in the apostolic anointing. Let's look at how the fivefold ministry was expressed through the life of Jesus:

1. Jesus Is the Apostle

"Therefore, holy brethren, partakers of the heavenly calling, consider the Apostle and High Priest of our confession, Christ Jesus" (Heb. 3:1 NKJV). The word apostle means "a sent one". Jesus was sent by the Father to reveal His heart and reconcile us back to God (John 3:16). He was sent to plant the Kingdom of God in this world and start a movement that changes the world. Jesus is the Apostle.

2. Jesus Is the Prophet

"And they took offense at Him. But Jesus said to them, "A prophet is not dishonored except in his hometown and in his own household" (Matt. 13:57 NASB). Jesus referred to Himself as a prophet. The prophet reveals the heart of God through revelation. Jesus revealed both the heart of the Father and His plan to save the world through Jesus. He came to declare the end of the old covenant era and bring us into the New Covenant. Jesus is the Prophet.

3. Jesus Is the Evangelist

"For the Son of Man came to seek and to save the lost" (Luke 19:10). Jesus came into this world to save sinners and to bring them back to the Father. Jesus' whole ministry was to a large degree focusing on preaching good news. Jesus preached the gospel of the Kingdom and healed the sick. Jesus is the Evangelist.

4.   *Jesus Is the Good Shepherd*

"I am the good shepherd. The good shepherd lays down his life for the sheep" (John 10:11 NIV). Jesus laid down His life for us and His heart was always for the broken and scattered people. The most common picture of leadership in all the Bible is that of the shepherd. Jesus walked in the fullness of this ministry. Jesus is the good shepherd.

5.   *Jesus Is the Teacher*

"Jesus went through all the towns and villages, teaching in their synagogues, proclaiming the good news of the kingdom and healing every disease and sickness" (Matt. 9:35). Jesus is an amazing teacher. The gospels are full of examples of Him operating in this ministry. He revealed the Father's heart and the nature of the Kingdom through simple and practical illustrations and parables. This is the essence of biblical teaching. Jesus is the Teacher.

As we have seen, the ministry gifts are expressions of who Jesus is. Since He now lives within you and me:

- **The Apostle lives within you.**
- **The Prophet lives within you.**
- **The Evangelist lives within you.**
- **The Shepherd lives within you.**
- **The Teacher lives within you.**

Jesus can flow in all these gifts through us, which means that all of us can be prophetic or apostolic believers. Since every spiritual blessing is ours in Christ, we have access to the full anointing of Jesus Himself.

Every Believer Is a Potential Ministry Gift

Because the ministry gifts reveal different aspects of who Jesus is and since He wants to reveal Himself through us, every child of God has the potential to operate in one, or even several, of these ministry gifts. The context where Paul mentions these gifts, seem to imply that the grace of these gifts has been given to each one of us. *"But to each one of us grace was given according to the measure of Christ's gift. Therefore it says, 'When He ascended on high, He led captive the captives and He gave gifts to people'" (Eph. 4:7-8 NASB).* Since we now have been made partakers of divine nature, all of us carries the full DNA of these ministries in our hearts, which means that every believer has the potential to grow in them. Our experience might tell us that not all believers will do that, but the potential is still there. Every believer can move in the grace of the ascension gifts.

Knowing that all of us carry the DNA of the ministry gifts helps us understand that there is nothing exclusive or spectacular with the ministry gifts. These ministries are expressions of Jesus. They are not offices, leadership positions or honorific titles. These gifts are job descriptions that come with a grace to equip the body of Christ. The reason that the DNA of these ministries are present within each one of us is that Jesus Himself is the ascension gifts. However, there is a difference between a believer flowing in the anointing of one of these gifts, compared to the believer who has grown into a mature ministry gift.

The Prophet and Prophetic Believers

We need to know the difference between the believer who moves in an anointing and a believer who has developed into becoming a mature ministry gift. I have observed that people often confuse these two, but there is a difference. We could use any of the five ministry gifts to illustrate this difference, but since the prophetic ministry is quite common in my church and network, I will use the prophetic for illustration here. We could define the difference between the prophet and the prophetic believer in this way:

- *The prophet* operates in prophetic ministry to equip the body of Christ to be a prophetic people, who flow in the prophetic anointing. All ministry gifts have been given the assignment to equip the body of Christ for ministry. *Some* believers develop into a ministry gift.

- *The prophetic believer* flows in the prophetic anointing and the gift of prophecy on a regular basis. They minister in the prophetic to the body of Christ and the world. This makes them prophetic believers. *All* believers are called to be prophetic believers.

Even though we used the prophetic as an illustration, this is true for the other ministry gifts as well. They are tools in the hands of Christ to equip His people and the goal is not to raise up ministry gifts, but for the whole body of Christ to operate in the full DNA of Jesus Christ.

The Believer and the Anointing of the Ministry Gifts

Since the DNA of all the ministry gifts is our inheritance and our birthright, it is possible for us to move in the anointing and grace of all these ministries. They are part of our new nature in Christ. To grasp what that might look like, here are brief descriptions of the believer who flows in each one of these gifts:

The Apostolic Believer

The word apostle comes from the Greek word *Apostolos*. It means *"a sent one"*. The apostolic believer is the pioneer who challenges status quo and breaks new ground and territory for the Kingdom of God. The apostolic believer is also a wise master builder, who builds new ministries and churches that reveal Jesus. They must embrace and operate in the other gifts to a degree. Usually, when a new Kingdom work is being built for God, the other ministries are not yet available. The apostolic worker must be equipped to do whatever is needed, until the other gifts have been raised up. The apostolic believer has a mandate to stir up the body of Christ to be pioneers and to create visions that advance our mission. They have a grace to train, equip and send people to pioneer the Kingdom of God. When we embrace our apostolic DNA, we will receive grace to take new territory and to pioneer new things for the Kingdom of God. We are apostolic believers!

The Prophetic Believer

The prophetic believer reveals the will of God and has a burning passion to call us into deeper intimacy with Jesus. The prophetic believer brings revelation and inspiration from heaven that help us discern the will of God. They reveal the heart of the Father, as well as His plans and purposes for the body of Christ. They point us to the heavenly vision that Jesus has for His bride. This is done through preaching, teaching, or prophesying. It can also be done through creative expressions, such as arts, dance and prophetic acts. The prophetic believer carries a grace to bring us deeper into intimacy with the Father and they have a passion for the body of Christ to grow in purity of heart and motives. When we embrace our prophetic DNA, we receive the grace to become a prophetic people. We are prophetic believers!

The Evangelistic Believer

The evangelistic believer is anointed to preach the gospel of Jesus Christ in a simple and captivating way. The evangelistic believer is the good news preacher who inspires and encourages the body of Christ. They have a passion to bring in the harvest of souls and inspire the body of Christ to spread the love of the Father. They carry a burden to reach the lost with the gospel and their ministry is usually accompanied with healings and miracles. Philip is the only person in the book of Acts that is called an evangelist (Acts 21:8). His example reveals to us what the evangelistic DNA is all about. When He preached *"… the multitudes with one accord heeded the things spoken by Philip, hearing and seeing the miracles which he did. For unclean spirits, crying with a loud voice, came out of many who were possessed; and many who were paralyzed and lame were healed. And there was great joy in that city"* (Acts 8:6-8). When we embrace our evangelistic DNA, we become bringers of the good news of Jesus with signs and wonders following. We bring in the harvest of souls by spreading the love of the Father and through preaching the good news of Jesus. We are evangelistic believers!

The Believer Who Carries the Heart of the Shepherd

The believer who carries the heart of the shepherd loves the body of Christ and is passionate for the well-being of the people that they are called to serve. The believer with a shepherd's heart will feed, instruct and guide the sheep. The shepherd is usually more of a stationary minister, who is serving and caring for the local fellowship of believers. These wonderful believers are filled with the supernatural love, patience and faithfulness from the Father. This enables them to handle the many challenges of serving the believers. The believer with a shepherd's heart carries a burden to help the body of Christ to love and take care of one another so that we can function in complete unity as the body of Christ. The best example of a good shepherd is Jesus Himself (John 10:11; 1 Pet. 2:25; 5:4; Ps. 23). Jesus is *the* Good Shepherd. By looking at Jesus, we will find the perfect model of the believer who carries the heart of a shepherd. As we embrace our shepherding DNA, we will live in our identity as the body of Christ and the Father's family. We carry the heart of the good shepherd!

The Believer Who Carries the Heart of the Teacher

The believer who carries the heart of a teacher is anointed to give revelation from the Word of God that reveals the heart of God and establishes us in Christ. These believers carry a passion to study the Bible and they are anointed to teach in a way that give insight and clarity into the Word of God. The believer with the heart of the teacher equips us to read, understand and teach the Bible. The biblical teacher is not a theologian, even though many anointed teachers still have a theological education. The teacher is equipped to teach the Word to the church in a way that imparts life from Jesus and reveals the Father's heart. When we embrace our teaching DNA, we become a people rooted and grounded in the Word of God. We carry the heart of the teacher.

You Carry the DNA of the Ascension Gifts Within You

As we have seen, the DNA and anointing of the ministry gifts are part of our inheritance as the Father's children. The conclusion of knowing this must be that because of the indwelling Christ…

- *We are apostolic.*
- *We are prophetic.*
- *We are evangelistic.*
- *We carry the Shepherd's heart.*
- *We carry the Teacher's heart.*

This is who we are as children of God. This is our inheritance and DNA. As we abide in the love of Christ, the DNA and anointing of these ministries will manifest in an effortless and organic way. The Father wants us to embrace these gifts as our identity, so that we can reveal the fullness of Christ to the world.

It All Belongs to Us!

It is powerful to know that we have full access to the DNA and anointing of the ministry gifts through Jesus Christ. They are our birthright as our Father's children. When we begin to realize that all belongs to us, we'll find greater freedom in our ministry. We will no longer look at the ascension gifts as either being present or lacking in our fellowships. They are present because of Jesus, even though they might not have manifested yet. *"So then, no one is to be boasting in people. For all things belong to you, whether Paul or Apollos or Cephas, or the world or life or death, or things present or things to come; all things belong to you and you belong to Christ and Christ belongs to God"* (1 Cor. 3:21-23 NASB). This way of thinking about ministry gifts simplifies the way we look at our ministries a lot. We no longer need to wonder what gifts we possess or lack. We are free to focus on making room for Jesus to express Himself in whichever way He wants through our lives. The essence of all New Covenant ministry is to allow Jesus to express His very own life through us!

Discovering the truths that I have shared within this chapter was so liberating for me. For the last twenty-five years, I've been part of a charismatic movement where most of the churches strongly emphasize a leadership structure built on the fivefold ministry. I appreciate much of the insights that this has given to me, as well as the diversity that the fivefold ministry brings. There are some religious traditions that has sneaked in with this emphasis on the ministry gifts, as well. For example, these gifts have at times been confused with offices, or even leadership positions. Even though it certainly is true that a person operating in these gifts can have a leadership position, a church doesn't have to be led by a team of fivefold ministries. The job of the ministry gifts is simply to equip the believers. They do that by imparting the DNA and life of Jesus Himself. In other words, these gifts are equippers, which is not the same as having a leadership position. These gifts have authority and wield influence, by serving the believers in love.

Another tradition that is common where there is a lot of focus on fivefold leadership, is that there is an emphasis on the believer who operates in one of these gifts. This is a very human centered way of building ministries, which often creates personality cults. However, it is important that we realize that these ministry gifts are always meant to be expressions of Jesus Himself. These gifts are not about the person operating in them, but they are all about Christ. As we surrender to the indwelling Christ, His very own life will be expressed through us and these gifts will operate in an organic way among us. It's all about the life of Jesus flowing through us, so that His DNA can be revealed through His body!

Activations

- Ministry is all about the indwelling Christ expressing His life through us. How does that revelation change your perspective on your ministry? Take some time to process this question together with the Holy Spirit in prayer. Write down what He reveals to you.

- Read Col. 1:27 and Gal. 2:19-21 together with the Holy Spirit. These are the two passages that we read in this chapter to highlight the revelation on Christ in us. Ask the Holy Spirit for more revelation on this topic. Write down any insight or revelation that you receive.

- In this chapter we saw that because of the indwelling Christ:
    - *You are apostolic.*
    - *You are prophetic.*
    - *You are evangelistic.*
    - *You carry the Shepherd's heart.*
    - *You carry the Teacher's heart.*

Spend 20-30 minutes in prayer to declare these truths over your life. Ask God to stir up these DNAs in your life. If you have a longing to grow into a ministry gift, ask Him to bring you through that process of growth.

- Which of these five anointings would you like to grow in the most? Where do you need to be strengthened? Ask the Holy Spirit how you can make room for Jesus to work through you in these areas. Ask Him to equip and strengthen you where you need to grow!

- Take time to pray and intercede for the body of Christ, asking Jesus to raise up more ministry gifts and for the DNA of these gifts to be activated within His body.

CHAPTER 6: WE HAVE BEEN ORDAINED BY THE FATHER

As we embrace our identity as children of God and tap into the creativity of heaven, there are some traditions that inevitably will get challenged until they eventually are thrown out. One of these being our view of leadership and authority, in the Kingdom of God. Jesus made some interesting statements on this topic that are so radical that they have either been forgotten, or even worse, being ignored on purpose. This has been a very common practice in the history of the church.

You know that the rulers of the Gentiles lord it over them and those who are great exercise authority over them. Yet it shall not be so among you; but whoever desires to become great among you, let him be your servant. And whoever desires to be first among you, let him be your slave— just as the Son of Man did not come to be served, but to serve and to give His life a ransom for many (Matt. 20:25-28 NKJV).

Jesus repeats this truth concerning how spiritual authority works in the Kingdom of God, in similar ways many times (Matt. 23:1-11, Mark. 10:42-45, Luke 22:24-27). It was very important to Jesus that His disciples gained a revelation on the issue of leadership and authority in the Kingdom. This was important, because the nature of Christ's rule is so completely opposite to the way of the world. Jesus rules in humility and grace. He radically redefines greatness and authority by showing us that true authority comes from the Father Himself.

Ministry Is to Do What We See the Father Doing

Jesus demonstrated what true authority and ministry looks like, through His own life. He revealed that His mandate to serve us came directly from His relationship with the Father. *"Very truly I tell you, the Son can do nothing by himself; he can do only what he sees his Father doing, because whatever the Father does the Son also does"* *(John 5:19 NIV)*. Jesus had no formal training for ministry and He hadn't been ordained by the religious leadership of His day. His only credentials were that He had been sent by His Father. Jesus did what the Father was doing, revealing the heart of God to the world (John 1:18). As Jesus commissioned us to go into the world with the gospel, He sent us in the same way that He Himself had been sent. *"Peace be with you! As the Father has sent me, I am sending you"* *(John 20:21 NIV)*. This is the basis for all type of ministry, in the Kingdom of God. Our ministry must always be birthed by a lifestyle of abiding in the love of the Father, where we allow Jesus to express His life through us. In the New Covenant, spiritual authority comes from our son-placing and from knowing that we have been ordained and qualified by Jesus Himself.

Hierarchal and Clerical Authority

Jesus had constant problems with the religious leaders in Israel over the issue of spiritual authority (Matt. 23:1-36). They had no revelation of the Father and their view of who should be allowed to minister was based on a religious hierarchy, where they were at the top. They held to a clerical type of authority, which was at its foundation, built on formal training and human credentials. Since Jesus hadn't received any formal theological training, they viewed His ministry as invalid or even dangerous. Their mistake was to believe that spiritual authority could be based on shallow things like titles, credentials, or theological training. This creates a hierarchal and clerical type of authority, which usually is how the secular and religious world views leadership. However, we must remember that Jesus said that authority works differently among the children of God.

We have been ordained by the Father and sent by Jesus to preach the gospel and extend the Kingdom of God. We have permission from heaven to do whatever God has called us to do. This is how the Kingdom operates and it will always challenge the religious system. Religious hierarchy and the Kingdom of God are totally opposite realms that can't coexist. These two realms are ruled by different spirits and governed by very different rules. Religious authority is always built on fleshly control and human strength, while authority in the Kingdom of God is built on Christlikeness and humility. The religious spirit will always persecute the one who has been called and anointed by the Father. This happened to Jesus all the time. The religious leaders constantly challenged Him and they did everything in their power to kill His ministry. We can find many examples of this in the gospels.

A Demonic Question

At one such occasion, a group of religious leaders came to Jesus with a demonic challenge. They confronted Jesus with a question that is commonly asked by religious leaders who feel threatened by a true anointing. This question is demonic, in origin as well as in nature, because it's based on fear and it is used in hierarchical structures to keep control over God's children. *Then he was back in the Temple, teaching. The high priests and leaders of the people came up and demanded, "Show us your credentials. Who authorized you to teach here?" (Matt. 22:23 The Message).* These leaders asked this question to undermine Jesus. They pointed out that Jesus never had been formally trained or ordained by the religious leaders in Jerusalem. Sadly, it was more important to these leaders that the one who ministered should be ordained by the right people, than if he was speaking revelation from God. To them, protecting the religious control over people was more important than receiving revelation. This is still one of the main reasons that there is such a lack of revelation within the body of Christ today. Jesus spoke about this when He confronted the religious leaders with these words: *"I have come in my Father's name and you do not accept me; but if someone else comes in his own name, you will accept him. How can you believe since you accept glory from one another but do not seek the glory that comes from the only God"* (John 5:43-44 NIV). If we are focused on titles and formal education as a basis for a true calling or ministry, we will lose a lot of valuable revelation and wisdom.

The Same Question Is Still Around Today

This same demonic question is still being used by every religious system to undermine and control people today. They might not use the exact same words but the spirit behind the question is the same. Every pioneer will have to figure out how to deal with this question. The motivation behind it is fear and its goal is to gain control over the body of Christ. If we put a system in place where the right credentials and education are needed to get permission to do God's will, we have nullified the headship of Christ. Jesus is the head of His body and He alone decides what His members are allowed to do. Jesus is Lord of His body and having received a genuine call from Him is all the credentials we need. Spiritual authority is always built on the Father's approval.

When the Only Right Answer Is to Ignore the Question

Jesus knew that they didn't ask this question from a pure heart. Therefore, He didn't answer them directly but instead gave them a question to ponder. *"I'll tell you by what authority I do these things if you answer one question," Jesus replied. "Did John's authority to baptize come from heaven, or was it merely human?"* (Matt. 21:24-25 NLT). By asking this question, Jesus revealed the true motivation of these religious leaders. They wanted to stay in control and be well-respected by the people, which is why none of them dared to answer His question (Matt. 21:26). Jesus was not interested in playing their religious game, so He never gave a clear answer to their question, even though the answer was glaringly obvious to anyone with even the smallest measure of spiritual discernment. *"So they finally replied, "We don't know." And Jesus responded, "Then I won't tell you by what authority I do these things"(Matt. 21:27 NLT).* We can learn a lot, by just observing how Jesus responded to this situation.

The Fruit Will Speak for Itself

When our authority or the validity of our ministry is questioned, it is rarely done with good intentions. It is usually done because people already have an opinion about our work. The best way to respond to such a question is usually to ignore it and to allow the fruit of what Jesus is doing through us to speak for itself. I have learned that it is impossible to win a religious argument, without getting into the flesh. People are free to have their own opinions, but our job is to do what the Father reveals to us. When we focus on that, the fruit of our lives will speak for itself. People whose heart have been touched by the Holy Spirit will see what God is doing. These are the ones that we should care about.

Ordained to Minister the New Covenant

It is enough for us to know that we have been ordained and sent by the Father Himself. We are now fully qualified to be ministers of the Spirit, within the New Covenant. *"Not that we are competent in ourselves to claim anything for ourselves, but our competence comes from God. He has made us competent as ministers of a new covenant—not of the letter but of the Spirit; for the letter kills, but the Spirit gives life"* (2 Cor. 3:5-6 NIV). We are free to operate with great boldness in whatever ministry or calling that we have received from Jesus. This is the sure foundation for all ministry in the New Covenant. Because we are in Christ, we are fully qualified to proclaim the gospel and to extend the Kingdom of God. This is the only valid ordination that is spoken of in the New Testament.

We Are His Kings and Priests

Where there are hierarchical and clerical structures of leadership, the positional view of spiritual authority will always follow. That kind of leadership structure are almost always built on these four components:

- Honorific Titles
- Offices
- Denominationalism
- The clerical/laity divide

None of these four components can be found in the Bible. Since we are His kings and priests who have been both qualified and sent by our Father, we don't need these honorific titles or offices.

But you are God's chosen treasure —priests who are kings, a spiritual "nation" set apart as God's devoted ones. He called you out of darkness to experience his marvelous light and now he claims you as his very own. He did this so that you would broadcast his glorious wonders throughout the world (2 Pet. 2:9 TPT).

We are His kings and priests and His intention is for us to preach the gospel all over the world. He has already qualified and sent us to do that. Sometimes, leaders can be tempted to find approval and identity through offices, or honorific titles, but Jesus plainly stated that it shouldn't be so among us. I'm not saying that it is wrong to give people a title, such as pastor or evangelist, which describes their function or their ministry in a church. I am saying that none of these are the basis for our identity and ministry. Our security, identity and approval are found in the love of Christ!

Authority to Serve People

Jesus tells us very clearly that in the Kingdom of God, no believer has formal or positional authority over their brothers and sisters. The only authority that we have, is the authority to lay down our lives to serve one another in love. People can grant us authority to speak into their lives if they trust us, but that kind of authority is not built on religious hierarchy, but only on trust. We do have authority over the realm of darkness and to heal the sick (Mark. 16:15-20). But in relationship to our fellow believers, our calling and mandate is to serve them in love.

From time to time, there are voices in the body of Christ, putting an emphasis on strong leadership and the restoration of five-fold ministry. I can appreciate that to a degree. There has been a much too narrow definition of what ministry is meant to look like and I believe that the ministry gifts are important for the maturation of the body of Christ. I do still have one concern and that is how some of the people calling for this, tend to look at leadership and spiritual authority. Jesus clearly stated that in the kingdoms of this world, authority structures are built so that leaders can rule and have authority over their people. He also said that it should not be so among us. No ministry has ever been given authority over God's children, but we are to use the grace and favor that come with an authentic call to serve the body of Christ.

Relational Authority

We have been given the authority to serve the body of Christ, but we can only minister to people when they trust us. As far as their willingness to trust us goes, is as far as we can minister to them. Therefore, all true authority in the Kingdom of God is relational authority. As we abide in the love of Christ, our love for other people will grow as well. This is not about us trying harder to love God and people, but about staying connected to the heart of

Jesus. It is by abiding in His love that we will find our place of spiritual authority. By loving God and loving the people, we gain their trust. That is the only way to minister in a way that has an eternal impact and that truly will touch their hearts. In this way, we can have huge influence on the body of Christ, even without having a formal position. Trust is the basis for true and lasting influence in the Kingdom of God.

It Is Now Easier Than Ever to Have a Platform

Since we are now living in this exciting era of internet and social media, all of us have a platform where we have the opportunity to influence and bless thousands of people. With simple tools like podcasts and the new, simple ways to self-publish books, anyone can have a voice. I consider this to be a huge blessing for us. We live in a time when it is easier than ever before to spread the love of the Father to the nations. We need many voices who preach the gospel by finding new, creative ways to reveal His heart. We live in a day of endless opportunities for the Kingdom of God.

Fear Is a Terrible Motivation

Sometimes leaders are afraid that if people are free to build their own platform and ministry, they will cause problems. Of course, that will be the case from time to time. Some people will use their platform to spread crazy ideas and bad teaching. But if we want to live as free children of God, this is a risk that we must learn to live with. We need to trust that the Holy Spirit has the ability to lead us where the Father wants us to go. His ability to lead us right is greater than the power of deception. Learning to trust in the Holy Spirit is a big part of what it means to live by faith.

The only alternative would be to create religious systems that we use to control people. The big problem with that is that this type of system will always be based on fear. Since Jesus will never use fear to control us, using religious fear and pressure to control the people we minister to, is a terrible idea. Fear is the total opposite of divine love and they cannot coexist. We must make the choice to either live with fear and control, or to abide in the love of the Father. If we want to live a Kingdom lifestyle, we need to trust that the Holy Spirit is able and willing to lead us into the Father's purposes.

Christlike Influence

As we have already seen, Jesus showed us what it means to live a life of true significance and authority in the Kingdom of God. If we live to find significance and greatness in this world, we will end up losing everything. But if our life's purpose is to know the heart of the Father, we will forget about such trivial things as our reputation, dreams of greatness and fame. By studying the life of Jesus, we behold God's description of living a life that matters.

Let this mind be in you which was also in Christ Jesus, who, being in the form of God, did not consider it robbery to be equal with God, but made Himself of no reputation, taking the form of a bondservant and coming in the likeness of men" (Phil. 2:5-7 NKJV).

This is the way of all ministry in the Kingdom of God. The Father will take us on a journey, where we will learn humility and self-giving love, resulting in our lives being poured out in worship of Jesus. *"And being found in appearance as a man, He humbled Himself and became obedient to the point of death, even the death of the cross"* (Phil. 2:8 NKJV). As the Father takes us on this journey of going deeper in humility, we will be rewarded just like Jesus was. True humility is the pathway to greater measures of grace and a life in victory.

Therefore God also has highly exalted Him and given Him the name which is above every name, that at the name of Jesus every knee should bow, of those in heaven and of those on earth and of those under the earth and that every tongue should confess that Jesus Christ is Lord, to the glory of God the Father (Phil. 2:9-11 NKJV).

The love of God will compel us to serve people with our gifts and talents, leading us to lay down our lives in humble love. This will always be the path to true significance in the Kingdom of God.

Activations

- You have been ordained and qualified to be a minister of the New Covenant and reveal the Father's heart to the world. Take 20-30 minutes in prayer, asking Jesus what this means for you. Let Him show you how this truth empowers your life and ministry.

- Ask the Father for more wisdom and grace to minister the New Covenant. Invite the Holy Spirit to reveal the religious traditions that you might be struggling with. Write down the issues He reveals to you and ask Him to lead you deeper into your freedom in Christ.

- In this chapter, we studied how authority works in the Kingdom of God from Jesus' words in Matt. 20:25-28. Spend some time to study and pray over this passage. Invite Jesus to reveal more to you on this topic. Write down the insights you get.

- What is the difference between the nature of authority and leadership in the Kingdom of God, compared to worldly authority? Pray and meditate on this question and ask the Holy Spirit for more revelation.

- Take 20-30 minutes in prayer and ask the Father to set you free from all worldly definitions of authority and ask Him to conform your ministry into Christlikeness.

CHAPTER 7: BROKENNESS, HUMILITY AND GRACE

There is a beautiful brokenness that the Lord wants to give to us as a gift. This is not the kind of brokenness that results from being wounded, neither is it the result of the pain from our broken past. This is the kind of brokenness that comes from knowing our need of the grace of God and our total inability to accomplish His will. Brokenness causes us to realize the deep truths behind the Lord's words of encouragement to the apostle Paul: *"'My grace is all you need. My power works best in weakness.' So now I am glad to boast about my weaknesses, so that the power of Christ can work through me"* (2 Cor. 12:10 NLT). It doesn't come natural for our flesh to depend on the grace of God, so the Holy Spirit must teach us how to do that. The Father already has a plan ready, through which He has ordained life to break our trust in our own ability and talents. He will put us in difficult circumstances, bring us through trials and mold us through challenging relationships to reach this goal. The result of this kind of brokenness is Christlikeness and a humility which keeps us moldable in the hands of the Father.

What Is the Good Kind of Brokenness?

Here is a good definition of brokenness: *Brokenness is the fruit of the Holy Spirit's transforming work in the life of the believer.* His goal is to conform us into the image of His Son. God is not the source behind everything that happens in our lives, but our Father will use all things and every circumstance to accomplish His work in us. *"And we know that all things work together for good to them that love God, to them who are the called according to his purpose. For whom he did foreknow, he also did predestinate to be conformed to the image of his Son, that he might be the firstborn among many brethren"* (Rom.

8:28-29). Our Father will never stop or give up, until He sees the fruit that He is after in our lives. That fruit is true Christlikeness. I have seen how He has used the trials and challenges in my life to conform me to the image of Christ. Even though these seasons were both challenging and painful, the result has been beautiful. The Father has made a crown of beauty out of my ashes and He has found a way to make Jesus shine forth through my pain.

Faith Tested and Purified by Fire

We have already seen how brokenness is the fruit of the work of the Holy Spirit, but it can also be the result of our surrender and the sacrifices we make to fulfill our call and destiny in Christ. The fruit of true brokenness is deep humility and us being moldable to the Father's dealings and plans. Peter speaks of this kind of brokenness as faith that has been both tested and purified by the fire. Our faith must be tested *"… so that the genuineness of your faith, which is much more precious than gold which is perishable, even though tested and purified by fire, may be found to result in [your] praise and glory and honor at the revelation of Jesus Christ"* (1 Pet. 1:6-7 AMP). There is a heavenly glory resting on the believer whose faith has been tried by fire. I have always felt a deep connection and unity in spirit with these brothers and sisters. I always leave renewed and refreshed after spending time with them. The sweet fragrance of Christ rests upon them and the fruit of the Spirit fills their life.

Seasons of Brokenness

The Father has ordained seasons of breaking for us. All of us will go through such seasons as long as we live. These seasons will at times be painful and challenging for us, but the good news is that they bear good fruit in us. I have seen how this works in my life on several occasions. As the Father is about to bring me into new seasons of blessing and fruitfulness, those are usually preceded by seasons of breaking, where my faith is purified by fire. I have learned to love seasons of brokenness. They build character and they always cause me to be even more rooted and grounded in the love of the Father. This brings us to an important Kingdom principle: *Before Jesus does powerful things through you, He will do something powerful within your heart.* During these seasons, the areas in our lives that we have been unwilling to give to God will be confronted, so that our resistance to His plans is broken. This will make us moldable in His hands, so that we can be conformed into the image of Jesus.

The Cornerstone that Breaks and Heals

Jesus Christ is the cornerstone that both breaks and heals us. This is one of the beautiful paradoxes with our Savior. *'The stone which the builders rejected has become the chief cornerstone. This was the Lord's doing and it is marvelous in our eyes'… And whoever falls on this stone will be broken; but on whomever it falls, it will grind him to powder"* (Matt. 21:42, 44 NKJV). He breaks us to set us free from our fleshly patterns and survival strategies, so that we can live in accordance with our identity in Christ. When I have come out of a season of breaking, there is always a season of healing and rest. Jesus is the true physician of our hearts and He knows exactly what we need to be conformed into His image and reach our full potential in Christ.

Brokenness Transforms Our Character

Since the goal of brokenness is Christlikeness, being broken by God will transform our character to look like His. Moses is a very good example of this. When Moses still was a young man, raised by Pharaoh's daughter in the palace, it was said of Moses: *"When they had to abandon him, Pharaoh's daughter adopted him and raised him as her own son. Moses was taught all the wisdom of the Egyptians and he was powerful in both speech and action"* (Acts 7:21-22 NLT). Moses was raised to be a noble man in Egypt and he had become a powerful man with the world at His feet. After Moses had been gripped by the calling of the Lord, his goals and direction in life changed quite dramatically.

By faith Moses, when he became of age, refused to be called the son of Pharaoh's daughter, choosing rather to suffer affliction with the people of God than to enjoy the passing pleasures of sin, esteeming the reproach of Christ greater riches than the treasures in Egypt; for he looked to the reward (Hebr. 11:24-26 NKJV).

The call of God started to burn in Moses' heart. He knew that He was called to be a deliverer of Israel. He tried to accomplish this calling in His own strength but failed miserably. Moses killed an Egyptian man and had to flee into the desert. He lived as a refuge for many years, but during this time God brought Moses through a season of brokenness. Many years later, when Moses received the call of God again, he considered Himself unable both to lead and speak. Before God begun the breaking process in Moses' life, he was powerful in speech and action, but as a broken leader, his character looked like this: *"Now the man Moses was very humble (gentle, kind, devoid of self-righteousness), more than any man who was on the face of the earth"* (Num. 12:3 AMP). Moses became a humble, gentle and broken leader, who utterly depended on the grace of God. This is the Father's goal with our lives as well. He doesn't want to break us and leave us there, but He breaks us to rebuild us, so that the nature of Christ shines forth through our character.

The Danger of Unbroken Leaders

Brokenness is especially important when it comes to leadership. An unbroken leader is dangerous to the body of Christ, because that kind of leader will lead through the strength of the flesh. We saw that Moses failed miserably when he tried to accomplish the call of God in His own strength. The good news is that God could reach Moses before it was too late and transform His character. The unbroken leader becomes a much bigger problem when they can continue to wield their influence on the body of Christ, over a longer period. This almost always leads to them building their own empire, where they usually create a culture of competition and entitlement. That kind of culture lacks the grace of God and exploits and wounds the body of Christ. Since Jesus is a humble King, true leadership in the Kingdom of God will always be built on weakness and brokenness! For this reason, it is important to understand the huge difference, between worldly leadership and the nature of leadership in the Kingdom of God.

In the world, leaders are chosen based on talents, education and strength. In the Kingdom of God, these things are usually more of a hindrance for the Father's work with us. Jesus always chose people based on His grace. Because of this, it is easier for Him to work with our weaknesses, than to use our strengths. When we live in true brokenness and humility before the Father, He can redeem our strengths and talents to become assets in His hands. Since He has created us with these gifts and talents, He intends to use them for His glory. However, for our gifts and talents to become useful to Him, we must be purified from pride and self-confidence. This is one of the main reasons as to why we must go through these seasons of breaking. We become almost useless in the Kingdom of God if we operate in pride. It is the humble heart that attracts the favor of God.

Brokenness and Humility

Our Father loves a humble heart. He gives grace to the humble. It is not that humility earns the grace of God, but the humble man realizes his great need for that grace and is therefore more open to receive it. The grace of God is both His unmerited favor and His empowering presence (for more on this topic, see my book *Transformed by the grace of God).* This is the reason that God gives grace to the humble. When we walk in humility, we will attract His favor and as a result we will be empowered by His presence. The connection between grace and humility is so important to

God that He expresses this truth, although with different words, several times within the Scriptures. Here are some examples:

"… and all of you, clothe yourselves with humility toward one another, because God is opposed to the proud, but He gives grace to the humble. Therefore humble yourselves under the mighty hand of God, so that He may exalt you at the proper time" (1 Pet. 5:5-6 NASB).

"But He gives a greater grace. Therefore it says, "God is opposed to the proud, but gives grace to the humble… Humble yourselves in the presence of the Lord and He will exalt you" (Jam. 4:6, 10 NASB).

"Though He scoffs at the scoffers and scorns the scorners, Yet He gives His grace [His undeserved favor] to the humble [those who give up self-importance]" (Prov. 3:34 AMP).

If we walk in pride, we will be opposed by God Himself, but our humility causes Him to give grace to us. It releases His power to work on our behalf. Since Jesus is humble, He cannot work with pride. This is the reason that He brings us through the seasons of breaking, so that He can create a humble heart within us that is open to Him. It is then that He can do meaningful work through us in the Kingdom of God.

Looking for Brokenness and Humility

One of the most important lessons I've learned when it comes to choosing co-workers, is to look for a broken and humble heart. It is dangerous to choose people for a spiritual work, purely based on gifting and competence. The strength of man is useless in the Kingdom of God. It can only be built by His grace and God gives grace to the humble. For this reason, it is important to look for a broken and humble heart in the people that we work with. True humility always attracts the grace of God. This is the only way to build something that counts in the Father's eyes. I have noticed that most of the damages and problems in different churches and ministries comes from lack of discernment of a co-worker's heart. When unbroken people are chosen to lead, the fruit will never be good in the long run. We need many humble and broken leaders to arise within the body of Christ. If we want to build something that lasts, creating a culture of brokenness and humility is more than crucial. Humility attracts the favor and blessings of heaven!

Paul and the Process of Humility

Throughout his letters, Paul reveals how his process of growing in humility and brokenness shaped his view of himself as well as of his ministry. His self-importance diminished in proportion to his growth in humility. Here are three simple statements by Paul in chronological order that prove this:

- *Paul begins by saying that he is the least of all the apostles (1 Cor. 15:9).*
- *Paul later stated that he is the least of all the saints (Eph. 3:8).*
- *In the end Paul states that he is the worst of all sinners (1 Tim. 1:15)*

Paul ended up viewing himself as the worst of sinners. This does not imply that he didn't believe that he had been made righteous in Christ, but it was an expression of His deep awareness of how much he needed the grace of God. True humility and brokenness always deliver us from self-importance, so that Christ becomes everything for us.

Exposing False Humility

There is a big difference between true humility and thinking less of ourselves. True humility has nothing to do with us despising ourselves and our gifts. That is false humility, which is a disguise for pride. Religion thrives on false humility, because it makes us appear humble, while the heart remains unchanged. Paul stated that he was the worst of all sinners, but when he confronted the false super-apostles in his letter to the Corinthians, he stated:

Now, I believe that I am not inferior in any way to these special "super-apostles" you are attracted to. For although I may not be a polished or eloquent speaker, I'm certainly not an amateur in revelation knowledge. Indeed, we have demonstrated this to you time and again. (2 Cor. 11:5-6 TPT).

For there is nothing I lack compared to these "super-apostles" of yours, even though I am nothing (2 Cor 12:11 TPT).

These statements by Paul doesn't look as humble as the ones that were quoted in the previous section, but they are. These leaders had challenged Paul's authority and identity. It would have been foolish to allow that. Humility is to agree with God and He will never push us down. This is how we can balance brokenness and humility, with the revelation of us being the beloved and favored children of God. We walk in brokenness before the Father, while at the same time being holy and complete in Christ. We walk in humility before Jesus, while also enjoying a life of being favored and blessed, by our heavenly Father!

The Blessings of Humility

God has promised to give blessings to the humble. We can't earn these wonderful blessings, but they come with the grace that God gives to the humble. The Father promises many powerful and beneficial blessings to His humble sons and daughters:

- *The Favor of God (1 Pet. 5:6)*
- *The Empowering Presence of Jesus Christ (Jam. 4:6)*
- *Exaltation and Influence (Ps. 147:6, Jam. 4:10, 1 Pet. 5:6)*
- *Wisdom (Prov. 11:2)*
- *Riches, honor, life (Prov. 22:4)*

- *God hears the desire of the humble and strengthens their heart (Ps. 10:17)*
- *Justice (Ps. 25:9)*
- *Understanding and revelation of His ways (Ps. 25:9)*
- *Kingdom of Heaven (Matthew 5:3)*
- *The humble will be lifted up (Ps. 147:6).*
- *The humble are beautified with Salvation (Ps. 149:4)*

These blessings will manifest in the lives of those who are living in humility and brokenness before God. To walk in humility does not mean that we are to despise or minimize ourselves, our gifts, or our accomplishments. Walking in humility means that we're realizing our great need of the grace of God. Only by abiding in the Father's love can we do what He has called us to do. Humility and brokenness are pathways to receive more grace from God. With that grace, all the blessings and benefits of humility will be added as well!

Activations

- We have studied the life of brokenness in this chapter. Have you been through seasons of brokenness? What is God working on in your life now? Is there a pattern to His dealings in your life? Take some time in prayer to process these questions with the Holy Spirit. Write down any new insights you receive.

- Take 20-30 minutes in prayer. Let this time of prayer be a time where you surrender to the Father. Ask Him to do whatever needs to be done in your life. Ask Him to make you more broken and humble before Him.

- In this chapter, I mentioned some passages that shows how God gives grace to the humble These verses are:

  1. *Prov. 3:34*
  2. *Jam. 4:6, 10*
  3. *1 Pet. 5:5-6*

  Read these verses again. Pray and meditate over them and ask the Holy Spirit to give more revelation on the connection between humility and the grace of God.

- Read the list in this chapter where I have listed some of the blessings that is given to the humble. Then take time to do your own research on humility in the Bible. What does a humble lifestyle look like? Do you find more blessings of humility? Write down the results of your research.

- Take some time to pray and intercede for the body of Christ. Ask the Father to bring us into more humility and brokenness before Him.

CHAPTER 8: JESUS – THE AUTHOR AND FINISHER OF OUR FAITH

Faith is a necessary ingredient if we want to fulfill a calling from God. Our heavenly Father is the ultimate believer. Since we are His children created in the image of Christ, we are now believers as well. We have been made partakers of divine nature and since God is a God of faith, this means that we have received a measure of God's own faith. It is important to know that the Kingdom of God operates by grace through faith (Eph. 2:8). Every blessing is given by grace, but we receive them by faith. Faith is the currency of heaven. This kind of faith is not a mere mental agreement with some biblical facts. That is not true faith. Faith is always built on revelation.

We can't drum up our faith through our own effort. Faith is a gift that has been given to us through the redemptive work of Christ. Faith comes by *"… looking unto Jesus, the author and finisher of our faith, who for the joy that was set before Him endured the cross, despising the shame and has sat down at the right hand of the throne of God"* (Hebr. 12:2 NKJV). Jesus Himself is a real believer and He now lives in us. Through His redemptive work on the cross, ever-increasing faith has become our birthright. Our part is to yield to the faith of Jesus, flowing through us: *"Jesus replied, "Let the faith of God be in you! Listen to the truth I speak to you: Whoever says to this mountain with great faith and does not doubt, 'Mountain, be lifted up and thrown into the midst of the sea,' and believes that what he says will happen, it will be done"* (Mark 11:22-23 TPT).

We Are Believers

We find several occasions in the gospels where Jesus rebuked the disciples for their lack of faith (Matt. 17:17-20, Mark. 6:14). There are examples of people asking God to increase their faith as well (Luke 17:5-6). However, after the day of Pentecost when the New Covenant was established, we find no more examples of this. The reason for that is that Jesus is sharing His own faith with us. This is one of the blessings of being in Christ. For this reason, we are now believers by nature. Lack of faith is not a problem anymore. Instead, our need is to receive more revelation of our inheritance in Christ. Since Jesus lives in us, we are believers by nature!

Unbelief Is a Choice

There are several references about unbelief in the New Covenant, but unbelief is not the same thing as a lack of faith. Unbelief is a choice not to believe, even when knowing the truth. We find the following passage in Hebrews: *"Take care, brothers and sisters, that there will not be in any one of you an evil, unbelieving heart that falls away from the living God" (Hebr. 3:12 NASB).* This implies that we can chose not to believe, while lack of faith means not having the ability to believe. This was the greatest sin of the religious leaders in Jesus' day. Even though they knew who Jesus was, they chose not to believe anyway (Matt. 28:11-15). Jesus faced the same issue in Nazareth. The people from His hometown refused to believe and their unbelief greatly limited the fruitfulness of His ministry. Jesus could only heal a few sick people there. *"And He could not do any miracle there except that He laid His hands on a few sick people and healed them. And He was amazed at their unbelief. And He was going around the villages, teaching (Mark 6:5-6 NASB).* Unbelief is a choice, but it is never referred to as lack of faith in the Scriptures. Jesus Himself is the author and finisher of our faith, which is the reason that our faith is always increasing and spreading!

Ever Increasing Faith

When the believer's faith is brought up in the New Covenant, it is usually referred to as an increasing and growing faith (Rom. 1:8, 16:26, 1 Tess. 1:8). There is never any reference to the believer's lack of faith. We have received the faith of Jesus as a gift and that faith is increasing and spreading through us. *"We ought always to thank God for you, brothers and sisters and rightly so, because your faith is growing more and more and the love all of you have for one another is increasing" (2 Thess. 1:3 NIV).* It is powerful to know that we have been born again as true believers and that Jesus shares His faith with us. This sets us free from the worry of not having enough faith. The truth is that it is impossible to have great faith if we focus on ourselves. True faith can only grow if we focus on Jesus. Our faith always comes from Jesus as a gift and it will only grow if we're beholding Him. This is perfectly illustrated by two very different people, who both had encounters with Jesus that transformed their lives.

The Key to Great Faith

There are only two people of whom Jesus said that they had great faith. At first glance, it might not look like they had anything in common at all. One of these two people is the Roman centurion. We read about His encounter with Jesus in Matt. 8:5-13. When Jesus saw the faith of this man, He was amazed. *"Now when Jesus heard this, He was amazed and said to those who were following, 'Truly I say to you, I have not found such great faith with anyone in Israel'"* (Matt: 8:10 NASB). The other person in the Bible with great faith, is the Canaanite woman. We read of her encounter with Jesus in Matt. 15:21-28. This is what Jesus told her, about her faith. *"Then Jesus said to her, 'O woman, your faith is great; it shall be done for you as you desire.' And her daughter was healed at once"* (Matt 15:28 NASB). These two individuals had almost nothing in common. One was a male, the other a female. One was a Roman centurion, while the other was a Canaanite mother. They only had one thing in common: *They were both gentiles.* This means that they were not under the law, so their faith had to be fully placed in Jesus alone. This is the simple, but very powerful key to great faith.

It is impossible to have great faith if we live under the burden of the law. Legalism always makes us self-centered and if we look at ourselves honestly, we will quickly come to the realization that we don't have enough faith for even the smallest miracle. But the Canaanite woman and the Roman centurion were not under the law. For this reason, their faith was placed in Jesus alone. As we have seen, this is the key to great faith. When we focus on Jesus, our faith will always be growing. This principle will never fail. We will always have great faith when we focus on Jesus. The faith of Jesus is the only faith that can move mountains and He now live within us, sharing His faith with us. This is the key to mountain-moving faith that releases miracles!

Hebrews 11

In Hebrews 11, we find the great chapter of the heroes of faith. This chapter reveals what the faith of God can look like in the life of the believer. This is a very fascinating chapter, which recounts many of the powerful actions that the men and women of God in the Old Testament did, because of their faith in God. This chapter basically illustrates the faith of Jesus in action, by using some Old Testament heroes to show us what His faith looks like, when it is flowing through us today. There are two important passages in this chapter that help us understand the essence of true faith:

"Now faith is the certainty of things hoped for, a proof of things not seen" (Hebr. 11:1 NASB).

"And without faith it is impossible to please Him, for the one who comes to God must believe that He exists and that He proves to be One who rewards those who seek Him" (Hebr. 11:6 NASB).

Faith gives us certainty about things that we hope for and it gives assurance of the things that we have not yet seen. When we live by the faith of Jesus, we know that everything God has promised is yes and amen in Christ. Without faith we cannot please God, but when we live by faith, we have bold assurance that the Father will reward us. We will now do a study of the faith of Jesus, by going through Hebrews 11. I suggest that you take time to read through that whole chapter before you continue.

Expressions of Faith in Hebrews 11

We find some important characteristics of the faith of Jesus listed in Hebrews 11. We are going to look at them now and as we do, we will see how important faith is when it comes to building our life and vision with Jesus. If we forget that this is a chapter about the faith of Jesus, we could easily become a bit overwhelmed by all the dramatic manifestations of faith listed there. It could cause us to feel like we don't measure up. Luckily, this chapter isn't talking about our own faith. This chapter speaks about the faith of Jesus flowing through us. This is what faith does:

Faith Gives True Understanding (Hebr. 11:3)

It is only by walking in faith that we gain true understanding of the character and ways of our heavenly Father, as well as of our calling and vision. The key to gain biblical understanding is not found in possessing knowledge of the Scriptures. The key to true understanding and insight is found in the revelation that we gain from walking by faith. Paul expresses this truth in the following simple, but profound way: *"So we fix our eyes not on what is seen, but on what is unseen, since what is seen is temporary, but what is unseen is eternal" (2 Cor. 4:18 NIV)*. Faith will open our inner eyes and give true understanding, which is why Jesus has called us to live by faith, not by sight (2 Cor. 5:7).

Faith Sacrifices (Hebr. 11:4, 17-18)

Faith sacrifices in a way that pleases God. Hebrews 11 uses Abel and Abraham to illustrate this. Abel sacrificed an animal by faith. The sacrifice itself was not what caught God's attention, but the faith Abel expressed in bringing the sacrifice did (Gen. 4:1-5). Abraham was prepared to sacrifice Isaac, his son of promise. The faith behind his willingness to sacrifice even the promises of God was pleasing to God (Gen. 22:1-19). When we live by faith, there will come times when we need to sacrifice as well. Sometimes we must sacrifice things like our time, our money, or our reputation. When we do that, we catch our Father's attention and as a result, blessing and promotion will come our way.

Faith Builds a Life of Intimacy with God (Hebr. 11:5)

Faith is the key to build a lifestyle where we walk with Jesus in intimacy. Enoch was a man whose whole life points to this truth. His life is summarized in a few short verses (Gen. 5:21-24). Enoch was a prophet and Jude even quotes one of his prophesies in his letter (Jude 1:14-15). But the reason Enoch is a hero of faith is that he walked so close with the Lord that He finally decided to bring Enoch home early. He never died, but instead the Lord raptured Him into the heavenlies. *"Enoch walked faithfully with God; then he was no more, because God took him away" (Gen. 5:24 NIV).* When we walk by faith our lives will be marked by intimacy with God. We will be firmly planted in the heart of the Father and our lives will be fueled by the love of Jesus Christ. True faith always produces intimacy with God!

Faith Is Rewarded by God (Hebr. 11:6)

Faith is always rewarded by God. The rewards that our heavenly Father gives, are not given based on our good behavior. He gives us rewards based on His goodness and grace. Our faith pleases Jesus (Matt. 20:1-16). When we take steps by faith, we can expect to be rewarded by our heavenly Father. Our faith pleases Him! (For more teaching on heavenly rewards and the judgement seat of Christ, see my book *Partnering with the Love of Christ*).

Faith Builds (Hebr. 11:7)

True faith always builds something for God. Noah is the example here. In radical obedience to the Lord, Noah built the ark to save his family and all the animals of the earth was brought along as well (Gen. 6-9). Because Noah built by faith, God's purposes with the world could continue as planned. Living by faith will result in us building something for God. We might build family, work, or a ministry. We will certainly build up our brothers and sisters in Christ. The point is that faith in God turns us into people who builds in the Kingdom of God.

Faith Responds to God's Calling (Hebr. 11:8-9)

Faith always responds to the calling of God and Abraham is the perfect example of this. When God called Abraham to leave his old familiar life to take the journey into the place where he would receive his inheritance, he obeyed and left his old life (Gen. 12:1-4). We will study the life of Abraham and Sarah later, but we cannot study faith without mentioning this couple. When we live by faith, it means responding to God's calling to leave our old life to take the journey into the promised land. A lifestyle of faith is very exciting. We will constantly be living in renewal since the calling of God will take us into new places and circumstances all the time!

Faith Enters the Promised Land (Hebr. 11:9, 33-34)

By faith, we receive and enter our promised land. Abraham and Joshua illustrate this, but this will happen to every believer who walks by faith. Hebrews 11 declares that the heroes of faith, were people *"… who through faith conquered kingdoms, administered justice and gained what was promised; who shut the mouths of lions"* (Hebr. 11:33 NIV). When we live by faith, we will have authority to conquer the kingdom of darkness and take our promised land. We will shut the mouth of Satan, who walks around as a roaring lion. His accusations are silenced in our lives through trust in the blood of Jesus. Faith in God conquers the promised land!

Faith Provides Spiritual Sight (Hebr. 11:10, 22)

Faith provides spiritual sight and as a result, it will give birth to a vision from God. Abraham carried a vision of the city that God had built. This is referring to the heavenly Jerusalem, which is a picture of the body of Christ. By faith, Abraham could glance into the future and see the plans and purposes of God. Joseph had a similar experience. Faith provided spiritual sight, so that Joseph could see the exodus of Israel from Egypt. When we live by faith, we gain spiritual sight, which will birth dreams and visions from God. In that sense, we will be able to live in God's future, while at the same time releasing His plans and purposes here and now. Faith always provides spiritual sight and vision.

Faith Births the Promises of God (Hebr. 11:11-12)

Faith gives us the power to birth the promises of God in our lives. There are many good examples of this in the Bible, but Hebrews 11 mentions Sarah as an example. She had been barren her whole life, but because she believed in God's promises, she was healed. God made her fruitful and she gave birth to Isaac (Gen. 21:1-8). Through Isaac, Sarah was blessed with countless descendants, of both spiritual and physical descent. When we are living by faith, we receive grace to birth the promises of God in a powerful way. God's promises will multiply in our lives to bless multitudes of people. The apostle Paul revealed how he labored and gave birth to the Father's promises by praying for the saints in Antioch: *"My little children, for whom I labor in birth again until Christ is formed in you" (Gal. 4:19 NKJV).* Faith releases the power and grace to give birth to the promises of God.

Faith Causes Us to Be Strangers and Exiles (Hebr. 11:13-16)

Walking by faith transforms us into peculiar people in the eyes of this world, because it causes us to live a Kingdom lifestyle that is totally different from how people approach life in general. The values and culture of heaven looks so different to the world, that it causes us to become a peculiar people to them. We are now strangers and exiles in the world. Paul wrote these words: *"And do not be conformed to this world, but be transformed by the renewing of your mind, that you may prove what is that good and acceptable and perfect will of God" (Rom. 12:2 NKJV).* Being renewed according to the culture of the Kingdom transforms us into walking signs and wonders that confuses and attract the lost. Jesus referred to this in His prayer, when He said that we are to live in this world, but not to live of this world (John 17:14-19). Instead, we are to live by faith, which will cause us to become a peculiar people that must be living as strangers and exiles.

Faith Resurrects Dead Promises (Hebr. 11:17-19, 35)

Faith will never accept losing the promises of God. Even if these promises must pass through death, faith believes in resurrection. This was the reason that Abraham knew that even if Isaac would die, God would be able to resurrect Him from the dead. When we live by faith, we'll be able to speak life even into the promises that look dead. We will live in the power of Jesus' resurrection, which brings the promises of God back from death. Sometimes our dreams and visions appear to be dying. During seasons like that, it's easy to just give up. But true faith will never give up and accept failure as the final word. Faith always resurrects the dead promises and brings new life!

Faith Blesses (Hebr. 11:20-21)

Faith releases the Father's blessings and we have been blessed to
be a blessing. Declarations of blessing releases the anointing and
spiritual power when spoken by faith. To bless people is to speak
words that impart destiny and transform lives, which is so very
powerfully illustrated when Isaac blessed Jacob, as well as when
Jacob blessed the sons of Joseph. For this reason, we are called to
declare blessings over people every time we get a chance. *"Never
retaliate when someone treats you wrongly, nor insult those who insult
you, but instead, respond by speaking a blessing over them—because a
blessing is what God promised to give you"* (1 Pet. 3:9 TPT). When
we walk by faith, we can declare blessings of heaven that impart
destiny and release the power of God, both in the body of Christ
and the world!

Faith Overcomes Persecution (Hebr. 11:23-27, 35-38)

Every believer will sooner or later be persecuted, but faith is the
victory that overcomes this world. By faith in the love of God, we
overcome all persecution that comes our way. Hebrews 11 points
to Moses as an illustration of this. Moses was raised to be part of
the royal family of Egypt, but he rejected the privileges of a royal
lifestyle because he considered the reproach of Christ as a greater
treasure. When we live by faith, we will sometimes be persecuted
and maybe even lose our reputation in the eyes of the world. But
the faith of Jesus always overcomes this world (1 John 5:4). Faith
in God will cause us to triumph during persecution and trials!

Faith Celebrates the Finished Work of Jesus Christ (Hebr. 11:28)

New Covenant faith always celebrates the finished work of Jesus
and it puts its trust fully in the blood. We find a prophetic picture
of this in Moses, who kept the Passover and sprinkled the blood
of the Lamb on the door posts of the people. Through the blood
of the Lamb, Israel was protected from the destroyer and found

deliverance from the slavery of Egypt. Jesus is our Passover lamb in the New Covenant and we have the privilege to celebrate His victory every day (1 Cor. 5:7-8). When we trust in His blood and declare His victory, we will overcome the devil. *"They conquered him completely through the blood of the Lamb and the powerful word of his testimony. They triumphed because they did not love and cling to their own lives, even when faced with death"* (Rev. 12:11 TPT). When we live by faith, we will boldly celebrate and declare the finished work of Christ and the power of His blood!

Faith Releases Miracles and Deliverance (Hebr. 11:29)

Faith parts the seas and moves the mountains to release miracles and deliverance from heaven. Right after the people of God had celebrated the Passover, they were delivered from the slavery of Egypt. When we live by faith, our Father will use us to break off oppression and demonic bondages. We will walk in the miracle power of Jesus Christ that restores broken lives. Our faith in God always releases miracles and deliverance!

Faith Takes Cities for Jesus (Hebr. 11:30-31)

Faith gives us the power to take cities for Jesus Christ. The people of Israel marched around Jericho until the walls surrounding the city fell. They then proceeded to conquer the city of Jericho. The strongholds and walls of unbelief that presently hold cities in bondage to the realm of darkness, will fall as believers arises to preach the gospel. Phillip shows us how to take cities for Jesus. As he preached Jesus in Samaria: *"Many evil spirits were cast out, screaming as they left their victims. And many who had been paralyzed or lame were healed. So there was great joy in that city"* (Acts. 8:7-8 *NLT*). When we live by faith, we will see whole cities and nations transformed by the gospel. Faith takes cities for Jesus!

We Have Something Better

All these manifestations of faith are very powerful and the deeds done by the people described here are astonishing. Yet, the Bible reveals that these heroes of faith longed for our day. They tasted the Kingdom of God and they saw glimpses of the greater glory of the New Covenant. But we have been blessed with the fullness of everything that they longed for.

These were the true heroes, commended for their faith, yet they lived in hope without receiving the fullness of what was promised them. But now God has invited us to live in something better than what they had—faith's fullness! This is so that they could be brought to finished perfection alongside of us (Hebr. 11:39-40 TPT).

We are living in the fullness of faith, because we have the faith of Jesus within us. We are living in the days of greater glory right now! All these heroes of faith would have given anything to be able to experience our day. We truly live in an amazing time!

The Faith of Christ Through Us

It might be a bit overwhelming to read about these powerful acts and lives shaped by faith in God, but we need to remember that this is not about our faith. Hebrews 11 was written to reveal what the faith of Jesus Himself can accomplish through the believer. Early in my life with Christ, I used to have a lot of worries about my faith. If my prayers were not answered, either as quickly as I expected or in the way I wanted, I used to feel guilty and blame myself for not having enough faith to receive from God. That led to much condemnation, but when I discovered that I was called to live by the faith of Jesus Himself, I was set free. Living by faith is a life of rest. We trust in the faithfulness of Jesus and His faith flows through us. We will experience the manifestations of faith described in Hebrews 11, by abiding in Him. The gospel is good news!

Activations

- Jesus is the author and perfecter of your faith. He lives within you and me to share His faith with us. How does that change your perspective on living by faith alone? Take some time processing this question. Invite the Holy Spirit to give more revelation on faith. Write down any insight you might receive.

- Read Hebrews 11 together with the Holy Spirit. Start by reading the whole chapter all at once. Then, read it again slowly. When Jesus highlights a certain verse or sentence to you, pause your reading and ask Him to show more. Write down the insights you receive. Continue to read in this way until you've read the whole chapter. Repeat this activation a couple of times.

- Does the life or testimony of any of the heroes of faith in Hebrews 11 speak to you in a special way? Do you feel specially drawn to the life story of any of them? Take 20-30 minutes in prayer. Ask the Father for the mantle and anointing of that person to be released in your life.

- Take 20-30 minutes in prayer and intercession for the body of Christ. Ask the Lord to stir up faith within His body to a greater degree. Ask Him to reveal more on the topic of faith to the body of Christ and for the gift of faith to be released more often.

Part 2: Abraham – The Father of Our Faith

In this part of the book, we are going to study the life of Abraham and Sarah. Their story is a beautiful illustration of the theme of this book: *Sonship, Faith and Vision.* The life story of Abraham and Sarah is a prophetic blueprint for us as children of God, who live with a heavenly vision in bold faith. As we're studying their lives, we will find a couple who loved God and responded to His calling. Their life was not perfect, but in their story, we'll find many valuable lessons on how to build a vision and to live a life in covenant with God, fully dependent on His faithfulness and grace. This is not meant to be a chronological or historical study, but the point is to draw lessons on faith and vision, by studying their life story.

CHAPTER 9: THE FAITH OF ABRAHAM

In the New Testament, Abraham is called the father of our faith several times. All of us who belong to Jesus Christ are called the offspring, or the seed of Abraham. Paul expresses this clearly in his letter to the Galatians: *"There is neither Jew nor Gentile, neither slave nor free, nor is there male and female, for you are all one in Christ Jesus. If you belong to Christ, then you are Abraham's seed and heirs according to the promise"* (Gal. 3:28-29 NIV). The faith of Abraham is so special that all who believe in Jesus are called his offspring. In this chapter, we will discover what makes Abraham's faith so powerful. His faith was built on a revelation of God and that faith was credited to him as righteousness. Hundreds of years before the New Covenant had even been established, Abraham already carried a revelation of Jesus (John 8:56). Abraham trusted in God and we have received that same justifying faith through the new birth. *"Abraham, our father of faith, believed God and the substance of his faith released God's righteousness to him. So the true children of Abraham have the same faith as their father"* (Gal. 3:6-7 TPT).

Abraham Was Chosen by Grace

Revelation is spiritual sight. The key to the greatness of Abraham is found in the simple fact that he obeyed what he saw from God. When he was called by God, there was nothing special with him. He wasn't known for his righteous lifestyle, or any extraordinary deeds. When Abraham received his call from God, his name was still Abram. He was an ordinary, idol-worshipping gentile that God had chosen by grace. The calling of Abraham illustrates this very powerful Kingdom principle: *"For it is by grace you have been saved, through faith—and this is not from yourselves, it is the gift of God— not by works, so that no one can boast"* (Eph. 2:8-9 NIV). The only reason that Abraham's life story became special is because he responded to the calling of God by faith.

Revelation and Faith

As children of God, we have received the same kind of faith that Abraham possessed. This faith comes from a revelation of Jesus and it is the kind of faith that overcomes the world (1 John 5:4). The faith of Abraham is not a mere mental assent to theological facts. This faith can only be found through a lifestyle of intimacy with Jesus Christ. It is the relational type of faith that is accessible through revelation. We always need the Holy Spirit to illuminate our hearts to reveal more of who Jesus is. Faith can never come by religious striving but is born in our heart as a gift of grace. As we have already seen, Jesus is the author and finisher of our faith, who now shares His faith with us. *"We look away from the natural realm and we focus our attention and expectation onto Jesus who birthed faith within us and who leads us forward into faith's perfection"* *(Hebr. 12:2).* Therefore, the flavor of faith is rest.

We Are Heirs of the World

To walk in this kind of faith comes with a promise that empowers everyone, who wants to preach the gospel of Jesus Christ all over the world: *"It was not through the law that Abraham and his offspring received the promise that he would be heir of the world, but through the righteousness that comes by faith"* *(Rom. 4:13 NIV).* We have become heirs of the world through our faith in Christ. Jesus has inherited the world through the cross and we have been made His co-heirs. This is a wonderful promise. We have been given a full mandate from the Father to extend the Kingdom of God everywhere. The promise to inherit the world is part of our inheritance as sons and daughters of God. We have a rich Father who has blessed us with a huge inheritance, but this verse not only speaks about that. It reveals something important about faith as well.

Justifying Faith

The kind of faith that Abraham possessed was more than just a mental assent to certain theological facts. His faith was a faith of the heart that put him in right standing with God. It is a faith that justifies. *"So also Abraham 'believed God and it was credited to him as righteousness.' Understand, then, that those who have faith are children of Abraham"* (Gal. 3:6-7 NIV). It is faith from the heart that justifies and makes us children and heirs of Abraham. Paul expresses this truth with similar words in his letter to the believers in Rome (Rom. 4:3-5). In the Kingdom of God, everything is a gift of grace that we receive by faith (Eph. 2:8). We have been made righteous through faith in Christ. This means that we have a right standing with our heavenly Father. We are His favored children who have become heirs according to the promise.

Inheriting the Nations by Faith

One of the promises included in our inheritance as children of God, is the promise that the nations will be blessed through us. It is by walking in our inheritance as children of God that we can release the heavenly blessings that we have in Christ. That is how we inherit the world. We have received a heavenly mandate to preach the gospel and bring healing to the nations through Jesus. Paul reveals how living by faith gives us access to the blessing of Abraham and how that will bless all the nations of this world.
"Scripture foresaw that God would justify the Gentiles by faith and announced the gospel in advance to Abraham: 'All nations will be blessed through you'. So those who rely on faith are blessed along with Abraham, the man of faith" (Gal. 3:8-9 NIV). Abraham received this promise when God called him. We saw earlier that Abraham had not done anything special to gain the Lord's favor at all, so this promise was based solely on God's unmerited favor (Gen. 12:1-3). Abraham simply believed what the Lord told Him, which was all that God was looking for in him. Consequently, Abraham was both justified and blessed.

Knowing that we have a promise to inherit the nations is a key to remember, as we steward the visions and dreams that God has given to us. The favor of God is activated when we take steps of faith to align our lives with the will of the Father. His favor will provide all the strength, provision and wisdom we need to walk in the will of God. The Father's grand plan is that all nations will be blessed through Christ. He plans to bless His Son with a big reward from His sacrifice. This reward will be given to Jesus in the form of a huge harvest of souls from every nation. We have been called to partner with the Father to make that happen, by preaching the gospel and extending the Kingdom of God.

The New Covenant Operates by Faith

It is important to understand that we receive our inheritance by grace through faith. This is how we got saved and this is how we are to live our lives, by grace through faith. We could never earn the favor of God and neither are we justified by good works. In the New Covenant, everything is given by unmerited favor.

For what does the Scripture say? "Abraham believed God and it was accounted to him for righteousness." Now to him who works, the wages are not counted as grace but as debt. But to him who does not work but believes on Him who justifies the ungodly, his faith is accounted for righteousness (Rom. 4:3-5 NKJV).

Even though this is a basic truth, Paul was led by the Holy Spirit to remind us of how we are justified by faith in all his letters. The simplicity of the gospel contradicts both the ways of the flesh and the teachings of religion, but the gospel challenges our thinking as well. This world has taught us that "we get what we deserve" and that if we want something good to happen, we must work hard for it. Even though I have been teaching on the grace of God for many years now, I still need a daily dose of the gospel. Since both the flesh and religion promotes the lie that I will get what I deserve, I need daily reminders that I live by grace through faith.

Sometimes my wife even tells me that I should listen to my own sermons. I have discovered that every time I listen to the gospel of grace, something is shifting in my heart and my internal world is more established in the finished work of Christ and the love of the Father. In the New Covenant, we receive what Jesus has paid for and we are rewarded with the full wages of His finished work on the cross. In Christ, we inherit all of heaven's blessings (Eph. 1:3). Favor and breakthrough are ours by faith. We are inheriting the nations and extending the Kingdom, by grace through faith.

Religious Works Puts Us under the Curse of the Law

In fact, those who choose to trust in their own works to live with God, put themselves under a curse. The law is impossible to keep and it will always condemn those who try to live by its letters, which is the purpose of the law. *"For all who rely on the works of the law are under a curse, as it is written: 'Cursed is everyone who does not continue to do everything written in the Book of the Law.' Clearly no one who relies on the law is justified before God, because 'the righteous will live by faith'"* (Gal. 3:10-11 NIV). There is no freedom or justification to be found in keeping the law and we will never find peace by adhering to religious works. The cursed life Paul is referring to here, is a life under constant guilt and condemnation. That lifestyle will lead to a cycle of defeat and passivity. Living under the law is the very opposite of living by faith and the two can't be mixed. *"The law is not based on faith; on the contrary, it says, "The person who does these things will live by them"* (Gal. 3:12 NIV).

Redeemed from the Curse of the Law

We have now been fully delivered from the curse of the law. This means that we no longer must endure a life of defeat, where we are oppressed by constant guilt and condemnation. Through His redemptive work on the cross, Jesus became a curse for us so that we could live a blessed and Spirit filled life with our Father. Jesus became as we are, so that we could become like Him:

Christ redeemed us from the curse of the law by becoming a curse for us, for it is written: "Cursed is everyone who is hung on a pole." He redeemed us in order that the blessing given to Abraham might come to the Gentiles through Christ Jesus, so that by faith we might receive the promise of the Spirit (Gal. 3:13-14 NIV).

This is one of the scriptures that has been a key for me in my walk with God. In my previous books, I have written quite extensively about my struggles with religion and legalism, so I will not share my story here. But I want you to know that I understand what it means to live a life under the curse of the law. I worked very hard under the oppression of religion, trying to earn God's favor and approval, but I was never able to find the meaningful life with God that I longed for. When my revelation of the New Covenant grew, I began to realize that through Jesus Christ, I was blessed and favored by my Father. I already had access to the Spirit filled life and I could receive and walk in it by faith. Being rooted and grounded in the New Covenant, set me free to live a blessed and fulfilling life with Jesus. Life in the New Covenant is way better and more exciting than I ever dreamed of. We are free from the curse of the law!

The Spirit Filled Life Is Our Birthright

We have received the promised Holy Spirit as a guarantee of our inheritance. *"When you believed, you were marked in him with a seal, the promised Holy Spirit, who is a deposit guaranteeing our inheritance until the redemption of those who are God's possession—to the praise of his glory" (Eph. 1:13-14 NIV).* The Holy Spirit is the reason that we can walk in our full rights as sons and daughters of God. The only way for the christian life to work is by the empowerment of the Holy Spirit. He is to our life with Jesus, what gasoline is to the car. You can't drive without fuel in the tank. Neither can we live in the fullness of Christ and experience His life, without the Holy Spirit. It is by the power of the Holy Spirit that we exercise our full authority in Christ and it's by the anointing of the Holy

Spirit that we can extend the Kingdom of God in this world. This is the only way that the promise of us inheriting the world, can become a reality. As wild lovers of God, we need to walk in deep intimacy with the Holy Spirit, drinking from His living water on a daily basis.

Justified by Works?

Some of you might remember a certain passage from the letter of James, that some believers think is negating Paul's clear teaching on justification by faith. A lot of people have asked me about this scripture. This is what James wrote: *"But do you want to know, O foolish man, that faith without works is dead? Was not Abraham our father justified by works when he offered Isaac his son on the altar? Do you see that faith was working together with his works and by works faith was made perfect" (Jam. 2:20-22)?* At first glance, it seems like James is contradicting justification by faith here, but that isn't the case. The works of Abraham that James refers to here, happened when he was prepared to sacrifice his son, Isaac, on the mountain of Moriah. We need to remember that these events took place many years after God had declared Abraham righteous by faith (Gen. 15:6). Abraham simply acted on what he believed.

In God's eyes, Abraham was already justified, but his obedience proved that he was a righteous man in the eyes of man. Abraham was a friend of God, who acted accordingly. That is the hallmark of possessing a living faith. A living faith bears fruit in the form of living works that flows from our union with Jesus.

And the Scripture was fulfilled which says, 'Abraham believed God and it was accounted to him for righteousness.' And he was called the friend of God. You see then that a man is justified by works and not by faith only (Jam. 1:23-24 NKJV).

Living faith will always produce good works. The big difference between dead works and the living works of faith is quite simple to understand. The works of the law is always done to earn God's approval and favor, while the works of faith is an expression of our faith in God. The works of the law is done in an effort to gain a right standing with God, while living works are done because we are the righteousness of God in Christ already. They simply mean that we live out of our identity in Christ.

Acting According to Who We Are

Since living faith flows out of our relationship with Jesus Christ, good works are the fruit of abiding in Him. It means that we act according to who we are. *"The Spirit Himself bears witness with our spirit that we are children of God and if children, then heirs—heirs of God and joint heirs with Christ, if indeed we suffer with Him, that we may also be glorified together"* (Rom. 8:16-17 NKJV). We have been made the righteousness of God in Christ, so that we can reign in life and the world has become our inheritance. Since we are the Father's beloved, righteous and blessed sons and daughters, we can live righteous and blessed lives that transform the world, as we extend the Kingdom of God. Let's act on this truth by finding new creative ways to express our life in Christ and to preach the gospel with boldness.

Activations

- We saw that there was nothing special with Abraham before God called upon him. He was an ordinary man, who was chosen and called, purely based on the grace of God. You were chosen and called by grace as well. How does that insight benefit you? Take some time to reflect on this truth together with the Holy Spirit. Ask Him to reveal greater depths of this truth. Write down any new insights you receive.

- Like Abraham, you have been justified by your faith in Christ. You are the righteousness of God in Christ. Read the following scriptures together with the Holy Spirit and ask Him to reveal more on this topic to you:

    1. *2 Cor. 5:21*
    2. *Rom. 3:21-26*
    3. *Rom. 4:5-8*
    4. *Rom. 5:17-21*

    How does knowing that you are righteous affect your calling? How does it give you more freedom in your life with Jesus? How does it help you to walk out your vision together with the Father?

- We inherit the world together with Jesus, through the gift of righteousness. We have a mandate and mission to extend the Kingdom of God, all over the world. Take 20-30 minutes in prayer. Ask God to fill you with a deeper passion for missions and evangelism.

- We saw that the Spirit-filled life is our birthright as the children of God. Spend some time with the Father in intercession for the body of Christ. Ask Him to take us deeper into the Spirit-filled life with all its blessings!

CHAPTER 10: ABRAHAM'S JOURNEY OF FAITH

Every believer who carries a true vision from God, will sooner or later be compelled by God to take a journey of faith. This journey will bring us from well-known territory, into unknown land and from the land of safety into places of daring trust and risk-taking. It's a journey from the dry desert, into the blessed promised land. The journey that brought Abraham from his old life into the land of Canaan, gives us a very fascinating prophetic blueprint for this journey (Gen. 12:4-7). This journey, even though only mentioned in one short passage, provides some very significant insights. We are going to study this journey of faith in this chapter.

Driven by a Vision of Jesus Christ

The book of Hebrews reveals more of Abraham's motivation for traveling. He had no clue where the journey would take him, but he was captivated by a vision of the city that God had built. *"By faith Abraham, when he was called, obeyed by going out to a place which he was to receive for an inheritance; and he left, not knowing where he was going… for he was looking for the city which has foundations, whose architect and builder is God" (Hebr. 11:8,10 NASB).* Abraham had been called by the Lord and with that calling, he received a promise and vision as well. He knew what his life could become, when he responded to God's call by going to the place the Lord had given to him as his inheritance. This vision was burning in his heart. Because of this, Abraham was willing to let go of his old familiar life. He left his home, his relatives and even his own country to find the place which God had called him to inherit. In the spirit, Abraham already saw the glory of the New Jerusalem and the marriage of Jesus and His bride. *"Your father Abraham was overjoyed that he would see My day and he saw it and rejoiced" (John 8:56 NASB).* This gave Abraham strength and courage to move on with God.

Getting Out to Get in!

Receiving a promise or a vision from the Father has the potential to change our lives forever in a very powerful way. To complete this journey of faith, we need to learn how to view our lives from His perspective. That is the essence of having a spiritual vision. The Father shares His own view of the future with us and invites us to partner with Him, in bringing that vision into reality. When our vision becomes more real to us than our present reality, it will be impossible for us to stay in the same spot. Abraham had a firsthand experience of this truth, when God spoke these words to him:

Now the Lord had said to Abram: "Get out of your country, from your family and from your father's house, to a land that I will show you. I will make you a great nation; I will bless you and make your name great; and you shall be a blessing. I will bless those who bless you and I will curse him who curses you; and in you all the families of the earth shall be blessed (Gen. 12:1-3 NKJV).

Abraham had received some very powerful promises from God, but these promises were all connected to his place of inheritance. This was the main reason that the Lord called Abraham to leave his old life. He had to get out to get in. That applies to us as well. We will not reach our potential in God by staying in safe, familiar territory. This is the reason God invites us to a similar journey of faith. This is a journey into the depths of the heart of the Father, where He positions us to live in our heavenly inheritance. Such a journey doesn't necessarily involve us moving to another city or country, but it certainly involves a reformation of our hearts. Abraham's journey reveals an important Kingdom principle: *We need to get out to get in!*

The Promises of God and the Greater Perspective

The promises God that gave to Abraham, wouldn't just benefit him and his family, but their fulfillment would bless the whole world. To receive promises of this magnitude from God, requires both a huge vision and a very humble heart. These two are God's power twins for every lover of Jesus. To have a humble heart is to have a big heart and such a heart has room for God's purposes. Abraham had both a humble heart and his vision kept increasing as God was working with him.

Because Jesus is the true seed and offspring of Abraham, He is the ultimate fulfilment of all these promises. It is because we are in Christ that they will benefit us as well. *"Now the promises were spoken to Abraham and to his seed. He does not say, 'And to seeds,' as one would in referring to many, but rather as in referring to one, 'And to your seed,' that is, Christ"* (Gal. 3:16 NASB). We don't know how much Abraham knew about the Father's plan to bring these huge promises to final fulfillment through Jesus Christ, but we know that these promises were a source of encouragement and comfort to Abraham. Every promise and vision we receive from God, will always work toward the goal of revealing Jesus to the world.

The promise of God propels us forward on our journey, while at the same time revealing Jesus. This is one of the reasons why we need to keep God's promises alive within our hearts. They reveal our future. When we meditate and pray over these promises, we receive strength from God and a huge dose of heavenly comfort and encouragement as well. I gather all my significant prophetic promises into a file on my smartphone. I read and declare them over my life every day. This is a very good way for me to remind myself of my reason for being alive. It is wonderful to start the day by declaring the promises of God over my life and ministry.

Starting the Journey

God told Abraham to leave his old life behind to travel to a land that he knew nothing about. In fact, he didn't even know where he was going when he started his journey. But he knew that God would show him where to go. Abraham trusted God and started his own journey of faith. *"So Abram departed as the Lord had spoken to him and Lot went with him. And Abram was seventy-five years old when he departed from Haran"* (Gen. 12:4 NKJV). When God speaks to us, revelation is born. Revelation propels us into the journey of faith. When God speaks, His word always comes coupled with empowering grace, which enables us to take the necessary steps to align our lives with His will. When a believer is about to begin this journey, they will know for certain that they can't stay where they are, but they don't always know where the journey will take them. I believe that most of us have experienced something like this. It happens when we receive new revelation from God and suddenly, we realize that we can no longer stay where we are. Neither do we know where this journey of faith will take us. The only thing we know for certain is that we have seen the new thing that the Father wants to give to us and our only option is to trust Him to lead us there. It is a good thing to follow the leading of the Holy Spirit in this way. It will keep us humble and dependent on Jesus.

You Are Never Too Old

One important thing to notice about Abraham's story, is that he was seventy-five years old when he started his journey. He was even older when his son Isaac was born. This shows us that we're never too old for God. I want to encourage those of you who feel that you're too old and that your time is over. It is never too late to say yes to God's calling. Your story is not yet over. In fact, God wants to give you many fruitful years with Him: *"For He says: 'In an acceptable time I have heard you and in the day of salvation I have helped you.' Behold, now is the accepted time; behold, now is the day of salvation" (2 Cor. 6:1-2 NKJV)*. Now is your time to arise and shine for Jesus. It is trendy nowadays to talk about the need of raising up young leaders. Of course, it is very important to raise up the next generation, but at the same time, we need to remember that God does not judge us according to the flesh.

The Father always looks at your heart and if your heart is open, all things are possible, no matter how old or young you are. This is your time. The Father's calling has nothing to do with age, but it has everything to do with your heart. If your heart is open for Jesus, He will do amazing things through your life. He wants to take you and me into the promised land. The Father will renew your youth and provide new strength (Ps. 103:5, Isa. 40:29-31). The devil is our accuser and one of the ways in which he accuses us, is to point out everything that is wrong with us. He will claim that we are either too young, or too old. He might tell us that we have the wrong education, or that we live in the wrong country or city. By trying to point out what is wrong with us, he wants to discourage us into giving up. But these things don't matter to God. He has already qualified us and ordained us to minister the New Covenant. This is our time!

Spiritual Sight Provides Endurance

The journey into our promised land will be challenging at times, but revelation provide spiritual sight. When we live with a vision or revelation from God, concerning His purposes for our future, we'll find the strength to overcome all spiritual attacks and the circumstances we must face to get there. We began this chapter by reading from the book of Hebrews, but let's continue to read from that passage.

By faith he lived as a stranger in the land of promise, as in a foreign land, living in tents with Isaac and Jacob, fellow heirs of the same promise; for he was looking for the city which has foundations, whose architect and builder is God (Hebr. 11:9-10 NASB).

Even though Abraham had been promised to inherit the land, he lived as a stranger and a foreigner in tent, when he arrived at the land of Canaan. This was probably not a comfortable lifestyle for a man of Abraham's age, but he endured because he had spiritual sight and he was looking for the city of God. Abraham had a clear vision of this city in his spirit and that gave him strength beyond his years. The vision of this city represented the inheritance that the Lord had promised to give to Abraham.

The Journey Is Completed

Abraham and his company completed their journey and arrived at their promised land. This journey both started and finished by faith. *"Then Abram took Sarai his wife and Lot his brother's son and all their possessions that they had gathered and the people whom they had acquired in Haran and they departed to go to the land of Canaan. So they came to the land of Canaan" (Gen. 12:5 NKJV).* As we saw at the beginning of this chapter, this journey is only described very briefly, in one simple passage. But still, this was by far the most important journey Abraham ever went on. Most of the time, the fulfillment of the Father's biggest promises is connected to His chosen place, which we might call our personal land of promise. Like Abraham, we need a strong spiritual vision to complete the journey of faith. This is one of the reasons why it is important to live with a deep revelation of Jesus and the heart of the Father. The wonderful reward of seeing the plans and purposes of God coming to pass in our lives is worth it all!

Making the Promised Land a Place of Worship

When Abraham entered the land of Canaan, the Lord revealed Himself once again. God did this to confirm His promises about giving the land of Canaan to Abraham and his descendants:

"'To your descendants I will give this land.' And there he built an altar to the Lord, who had appeared to him. And he moved from there to the

mountain east of Bethel and he pitched his tent with Bethel on the west and Ai on the east; there he built an altar to the Lord and called on the name of the Lord" (Gen. 12:7-8 NKJV).

The Lord knew that Abraham needed to be reassured of God's promises several times. It is important that we keep the promises of God alive in our heart. A good way to do this is to write down, or record, the important prophetic words that we have received from Jesus. If we do that, we can read and listen to them again, which is a good way to keep God's promises alive within our hearts. The response of Abraham when he entered the promised land, reveals another important Kingdom principle.

When we enter our land of promise together with Jesus, we need to immediately make it a place of worship. Our vision is never meant to be place of strife and human striving. We are called to live in restful increase. The only way to fully possess our land of promise while being at rest is through a lifestyle of worship and intimacy with Christ. Jesus is our promised land, so we can only steward it in union with Him. Cultivating a lifestyle of worship will keep us rooted and grounded in His love and it helps us to keep our eyes on Him. The Kingdom principle to remember here is this: *We possess our land of promise by making it a place of worship!*

Continual Encouragement from Christ

We saw that as soon as Abraham entered the land, God began to encourage him by repeating that the land of Canaan was meant to be the inheritance of his offspring. One important aspect of the present-day ministry of Christ is to comfort and encourage us. This part of His ministry is illustrated in a beautiful way, by how He kept on reminding Abraham of the promises He had given to him. Abraham needed continual encouragement and he kept his heart open for the Lord to speak. To receive words of comfort or encouragement, either directly from the Lord, or as He speaks to us through other people is vital for us if we want to possess our land of promise. We need continual encouragement and comfort from the Father. (For a deeper study of this subject, see my books *Abiding in the Father's Love* and *The Burning Love of Jesus Christ).* The good news for us is that through our union with Christ, we now have access to an endless source of both encouragement and comfort from Jesus all the time. *"Look at how much encouragement you've found in your relationship with the Anointed One! You are filled to overflowing with his comforting love"* (Phil. 2:1 TPT).

Activations

- In this chapter, we saw how a fresh revelation from the Lord compels us to take a journey of faith. Have you ever had revelations from Jesus that have caused you to take a similar journey of faith? Are you on this kind of faith-journey right now? Will you have to take this journey at some point in your life? Take time to process this with Jesus. Write down any insight that you receive.

- I wrote that this journey of faith will take you deeper into the Father's heart. Take 20-30 minutes in prayer and ask the Father to take you into new depths of His love. Soak in His presence and abide in His love.

- In this chapter, we discovered this important Kingdom principle concerning entering the promise land: *You need to get out to get in.* What do you need to leave behind to fully possess you promised land? Ask the Holy Spirit for insight in this area. Write down what He reveals to you.

- We saw how we can possess our promised land in peace and restful increase, if we make it a place of worship and thanksgiving. Spend some time worshipping the Father, thanking Him for the vision He has given to you.

- We need continual encouragement from the Father. Take some time in prayer and ask Him to speak words of life and encouragement to you, in the following three ways:

  1. *Ask the Father for an encouraging bible verse.*
  2. *Ask Him for an encouraging personal word.*
  3. *Ask Him to encourage you through a vision or dream.*

Write down the encouraging words and visions that you receive from the Father and take some time to pray over them.

- Repeat the previous activation once again. But this time, ask Jesus to highlight at least three different persons that He wants to encourage. Ask Jesus to give a bible verse, a prophetic word and a vision/dream for each one of these three persons, as an encouragement.

CHAPTER 11: FAILURE, TRANSPARENCY AND RESTORATION

Every child of God who builds a vision or dream with Jesus, will sooner or later be confronted with their own weaknesses. This is inevitable. The Father has chosen to work with imperfect people like us and sometimes our imperfections will be brought to the surface. For this reason, we need to learn how we can process our weaknesses the right way. We shouldn't spiritualize, or make up excuses for our struggles, but neither should we ever allow guilt and condemnation to torment us. Just like Abraham, we need to let go of our failures and mistakes, so that we can move on with the Father.

The Failures and Mistakes of Abraham

It has been liberating for me to discover that almost all the people I read about in the Bible are so very ordinary. There is never any pretense of perfection or spiritual facades, when God writes our story. Our biblical heroes of faith were ordinary people, who had to deal with their flaws and struggles, just like you and me. This includes Abraham. In this chapter, we're going to gain important insights from Abraham's mistakes. Later, we are going to look at his and Sarah's most painful failure with Hagar and Ishmael. But here, we're going to study some other occasions when they made a mess of things and missed God's will. We're doing this to learn how to deal with our own shortcomings in the best way possible. Sooner or later, we will fail and the story of Abraham gives us many good lessons on how to handle our failures and mistakes.

Abraham Panics and Flees to Egypt

Right after Abraham had possessed his promised land, a severe famine hit the land. The Lord had promised to bless and always be with Abraham. It is obvious that God wanted to provide for him. Yet, Abraham reacted with fear and went to Egypt. *"At that time a severe famine struck the land of Canaan, forcing Abram to go down to Egypt, where he lived as a foreigner"* (Gen. 12:10 NLT). This is one of the challenges that we must face, when we build a vision for God. The devil has certain areas that he repeatedly will attack to steal or limit our vision. Attacking our finances is one of them. The reason that he does this so frequently is that it has proven to be so effective. If the devil can limit the inflow of finances, he can control our vision and to a high degree render us ineffective. He operates through ungodly control and controlling money is one of the major ways, in which he tries to oppress the body of Christ.

In the Bible, Egypt is a picture of the worldly system. This means that when Abraham came under financial pressure, he went back to the ways of the world to solve it. By doing this, Abraham left his God-given place of protection and provision. The wisdom of the world teaches us to survive by hard work and saving money. Of course, it is important to have a good work ethic and wisdom how to steward our finances. The problems arise when we try to create financial security without God. If we want to do that, our safety will become our idol. That's the total opposite of how the Kingdom of God operates. In the Kingdom, our security is found in Christ alone. The Father's plan to provide for us is through the principle of sowing and reaping. He always has a plan to provide for us, but He will never force it upon us. God allowed Abraham to go out and try to find provision and security in the flesh, even if doing this created more problems for him.

Jesus Released Financial Abundance Through the Cross

The only biblical way to live in financial freedom and not giving in to fear is to live with a revelation of our Father's goodness and His desire to bless us. He has already planned for our provision. Jesus broke the curse of lack and poverty through the cross and He wants us to be blessed with more than enough. *"For you know the grace of our Lord Jesus Christ, that though he was rich, yet for your sake he became poor, so that you through his poverty might become rich.)" (2 Cor. 8:9 NIV).* We need to be rooted and grounded in the truth that Jesus released the riches of heaven through the cross. We can fully trust in His plans to provide for us. This revelation imparts strength and courage to us, so that we can stand firm in our vision and calling, even though we sometimes must endure seasons of lack and famine.

Abraham Lies and Sacrifices His Wife to Protect Himself

If we allow fear to bind us in one area, it usually spreads to other areas as well. Not only did Abraham walk in fear because of this famine, but he feared that his beautiful wife, Sarah, would draw him into trouble as well.

As he was approaching the border of Egypt, Abram said to his wife, Sarai, "Look, you are a very beautiful woman. When the Egyptians see you, they will say, 'This is his wife. Let's kill him; then we can have her!' So please tell them you are my sister. Then they will spare my life and treat me well because of their interest in you (Gen. 13:11-13 NLT).

The book of Proverbs shows us that the fear of man brings a snare (Prov. 29:25). The fear of man is another one of the devil's most successful traps. If we get caught in it, our freedom and boldness to live out our vision will be limited. It takes the wildness out of us. Fear is a major weapon, through which Satan tries to control our vision and limit the effectiveness of our ministry. Sometimes, the devil masks fear as "religious wisdom". In such cases, there is an emphasis on not taking risks that will make us look foolish if we fail. There will also be a focus on the church being seeker sensitive and respectable, so that unbelievers don't get offended by our behavior. That is the culture of religion, but not the values of the Kingdom of God. We are a peculiar people that the world will never fully understand. There is great freedom to be found in coming to terms with that! We shouldn't try to act weird and become unrelatable to other people, but neither should we try to be a church that embraces the expectations of this world. We are called to reflect Jesus and be conformed into His image!

Fear Is a Self-fulfilling Prophecy

Fear is like a self-fulfilling prophecy. Soon, Abraham's worst fear became his reality. *"And sure enough, when Abram arrived in Egypt, everyone noticed Sarai's beauty. When the palace officials saw her, they sang her praises to Pharaoh, their king and Sarai was taken into his palace" (Gen. 12:14-15 NLT).* Pharaoh's people brought Sarah into his palace and he even sent valuable gifts to Abraham because of this (Gen. 12:16). This shows us that sometimes, it might look like walking in fear comes with its own rewards, but fear has never been a tool that God uses to bless us. In fact, Abraham's stupid and fearful choices, brought a severe plague upon the Egyptians. It was only after Pharaoh handed Sarah back to Abraham again and sent them away from the land that the torment ended (Gen. 12:17-20). Every child of God needs to learn to let Jesus be their defender. We should never sacrifice our own people to protect ourselves. This is even more important if God has called you to build a vision. We are called to trust in the Lord for protection, not try to protect ourselves, through lies and half trues. This was apparently a very hard lesson for Abraham to learn.

Abraham Repeats His Mistake

Many years later, Abraham repeated this same mistake by telling king Abimelech that Sarah was his sister (Gen. 20:1-2). The king brought Sarah into his palace. This time, God saved Abraham by visiting the king in a dream. *"But God came to Abimelech in a dream of the night, and said to him, "Behold, you are a dead man because of the woman whom you have taken, for she is married." Now Abimelech had not come near her; and he said, "Lord, will You kill a nation, even though blameless?"(Gen. 20:3-4 NASB)?* When Abimelech told his servants what had happened, they became totally terrified and they quickly handed Sarah back to Abraham again (Gen 20:5-16). Abimelech had acted in good faith toward Sarah, but Abraham's lie had serious consequences. All the women in the house of king Abimelech had become barren because of this, but Abraham was led to pray for them to be restored. They were healed and the barrenness was taken away.

Then Abraham prayed to God and God healed Abimelek, his wife and his female slaves so they could have children again, for the Lord had kept all the women in Abimelek's household from conceiving because of Abraham's wife Sarah (Gen. 20:17-18 NLT).

This is a wild story. I wonder how Sarah felt while all of this was going on. This was the second time she had been handed over to a gentile ruler and brought into his palace, all because Abraham wanted to save his own skin. However, it is comforting to know that the Lord saved them, first by intervening through a dream and then by healing the barren women. Our Father is the God of the second chance.

Perfect Love Casts Out Fear

Our Father has provided a life of freedom from the fear of man for us. Abiding in His love will help us to cultivate a lifestyle of true boldness and freedom. *"There is no fear in love, but perfect love drives out fear, because fear involves punishment and the one who fears is not perfected in love. We love, because He first loved us"* (1 John 4:18-19 NKJV). The love of God and fear can't coexist. When the love of the Father invades an area of our heart, fear will be driven out of that area. As we keep on growing in His love, we will be set free to love and serve people without fear. We will then find the strength to stand firm in our vision, even if we must go through seasons of financial hardship and rejection. The love of God sets us free to be more than conquerors through Him who loves us.

Abraham Returns to the Promise Land

Our Father will always have a plan ready to redeem and restore us from our failures and sins. For Abraham, this meant returning to the land of Canaan. God had now blessed him with riches and he had become a wealthy man. *"So Abram went up from Egypt to the Negev, with his wife and everything he had and Lot went with him. Abram had become very wealthy in livestock and in silver and gold"* (Gen. 13:1-2 NIV). Earlier, Abraham had left his promised land for Egypt because of lack. This choice took him out of God's will, but God didn't give up on Abraham. God even restored him and blessed him in the area where he had failed in the past. It is worth noticing that he came back to the promised land together with his wife. Even though Sarah must have been hurt by Abraham's selfishness, their marriage was now made whole and restored.

Grace Abounds Much More

This illustrates an important biblical principle: *"But where sin abounded, grace did much more abound: that as sin hath reigned unto death, even so might grace reign through righteousness unto eternal life by Jesus Christ our Lord"* (Rom. 5:20-21). In our areas of failure and sin, our Father wants His grace to abound much more, so that we can be restored. This will transform our areas of brokenness into areas of healing and blessing. Abraham returned to the place of worship and blessing to get a renewed revelation of God. *"From the Negev he went from place to place until he came to Bethel, to the place between Bethel and Ai where his tent had been earlier and where he had first built an altar. There Abram called on the name of the Lord"* (Gen. 13:3-4 NIV). The powerful Kingdom principle to remember here is this one: *Where sin has abounded in your life, the grace of God will always abound much more.* Jesus always has a plan ready for us to be restored when we sin and fail, or when others have failed and sinned against us. The Father took our stupidity factor into the equation when He saved us!

Fear Blinds Us to God's Reality

We have seen how fear was the root cause of most of Abraham's bad decisions. Since Abraham had been called by God to become the father of faith, the devil wanted to create strongholds of fear in his life. The good news is that Abraham didn't give in to fear, but he found a way to overcome and grow in faith. The plan of the devil will always be the very opposite of God's purposes for your life. For example, I personally know many people who have been called to healing ministry. Most of them have had to fight long and hard battles with sickness. Other friends have been called to teach the body of Christ about prosperity and how to steward finances. Most of these friends have been delivered from a life in bondage to poverty and debt.

The Trap of Public Perception

As children of God, we have been called to break out of religious boxes and take new territories for the Kingdom of God. This can be a lonely path at times, where we will face a lot of rejection and criticism. All of us have a need to be accepted and loved. We will sometimes be tempted to become more politically correct, just to gain the approval of the religious world. I call this temptation the trap of public perception. This might be the greatest challenge of all for us to overcome. The burden of trying to live up to public perception by wanting to appear better, or more successful than we really are, becomes a heavy burden to bear. A tragic result of living like that is that we will never be loved for who we are, but only for the person we pretend to be. If public perception become our identity, we will be known only by our public image. That is a very lonely place to be stuck in and the torment of loneliness in leadership, has almost become a pandemic today. The reason for this is that religion always encourages its leaders to work on the public persona and appearance.

When public perception becomes more important to us than who we really are, our lives become very superficial. It is impossible to build relationships with depth that way, because to do so, we need to let people know who we really are. We have already seen that our Father is a relational God who is interested in our hearts. The heart is the core of who we are, the real us. The real us is the only version of us that God is interested in. He can't love or bless our public self, because it is not real. He will only meet us where we are and work with the real us. It is the devil who is interested in appearing better than he really is. Since Satan is the god of this age, our culture reflects his nature (2 Cor. 4:4). The good news is that our Father knows everything about our lives, including our weaknesses and failures and He loves us anyway.

Authenticity and Freedom

Powerful things happen when we are vulnerable and authentic with one another. We can admire someone whom we perceive as a perfect and invulnerable believer, but we could never relate to them. All of us certainly know that we are not perfect and neither are we invulnerable. Therefore, we can easily relate to the person who is struggling with pain and wounds, because we do too. The religious world values a good appearance and human order, but building a vision with God will sometimes make us look foolish. In fact, pioneering new things will become quite messy at times. Therefore, as children of God we must learn to value authenticity and freedom.

Paul the apostle is a good example of this. We have already seen how he very openly shared his challenges, fears and weaknesses in his second letter to the Corinthians. In this verse, he explains why: *"If I wish to boast, I will not be foolish, because I will be speaking the truth. But I abstain [from it], so that no one will credit me with more than [is justified by what] he sees in me or hears from me"* (2 Cor. 12:6 AMP). Paul had experienced a lot of breakthroughs, which provided countless testimonies that he could use to hype up his ministry and make himself look better and more respectable. Just think of all the things that Paul could have done if he had gained access to social media, but he was not interested in doing that. Instead, he wanted no one to think higher of him than they did when they met him in person. When people sat under Paul's ministry, they met an ordinary human being. True authenticity will always be the path to true freedom in our life and ministry.

We Have the Treasure in Earthen Vessels

In the same letter to the Corinthians, Paul gives us a glimpse of how he was able to live in the tension between the power of God and his own human weaknesses. He knew the power of God and walked in sonship to a higher degree than most. Yet, he was also aware of his weaknesses and humanity. This is how he describes what that looked like: *"But we have this treasure in earthen vessels, that the excellency of the power may be of God and not of us"* (2 Cor. 4:7). Our lives are a mix of tragedy and triumph, joy and pain, healing and brokenness. It is important that our life with God, as well as our meaningful relationships with our friends, has room for the pain and failures that comes with being human. Jesus is interested in our whole life and it is only when we allow Him to share our pain and sorrow that we can find healing and comfort.

It is easy to share our victories with one another, but the truth is that we can never have any depth in our relationships, until our friends have seen our brokenness and weaknesses. If our friends never get an opportunity to see us at our worst and still love us, we will never know how strong our relationships really are. I'm blessed to have people in my life. They have seen me at my worst and still love me. First and foremost, my family, but also friends and mentors. I am not afraid to end up alone if I would fail or fall into sin, because I know that my relationships go much deeper than that.

Abiding in the Father's Love Sets Us Free

The only road to true vulnerability and authenticity is to abide in the Father's love. As we learn how to live rooted and grounded in His approval and favor, we will find our value in Christ. That will deliver us from the need to appear better than we are. To struggle with weakness doesn't mean that we are bad believers. It just means that we are humans and as we are being set free from the fear of rejection, we can be fully transparent with our pain. Then our wounds will become a source of both healing and blessing. Every wound and failure can be transformed into a well of healing and restoration for other people if we give our pain to Jesus.

Identification and Compassion

As royal and blessed children who are part of the Father's family, we have been called to walk in compassion with our brothers and sisters in Christ. *"Rejoice with them that do rejoice and weep with them that weep" (Rom. 12:15).* This goes much deeper than human compassion. We are now His family and we have been made one in Christ. Jesus is the head and we are His body. We live in union, both with Jesus Himself and one another. The breakthroughs of our brothers and sisters in Christ are our victories as well, just as their pain and failures are ours to share. *"And whether one member suffer, all the members suffer with it; or one member be honoured, all the members rejoice with it. Now ye are the body of Christ and members in particular"* (1 Cor. 12:26-27).

As we get to know the heart of the Father more, we will grow in compassion with the whole body of Christ. If we want to minister healing to one another, we need to be compassionate people who love mercy. Spiritual maturity does not mean that we never fail, or that we will live pain-free lives, but it does mean that we learn to process our personal failures together with the Father, in such a way that He can use them to conform us into the image of Jesus. This is how *"…all things work together for good to them that love God, to them who are the called according to his purpose"* (Rom. 8:28). Since this means giving up control of our lives and trust in Jesus, it will require humility and brokenness before God. But doing that will set us free, both to celebrate and weep with other people. We will then be able to celebrate the successes and breakthroughs of our brothers and sisters, but we will also be able to mourn with them in their seasons of pain.

Jesus Still Carries His Scars

"Then saith he to Thomas, Reach hither thy finger and behold my hands; and reach hither thy hand and thrust it into my side: and be not faithless, but believing. And Thomas answered and said unto him, My Lord and my God" (John 20:27-28). Jesus is our risen Savior and Lord, but I find it comforting to know that He still carries all His scars. When we meet Jesus, we will still be able to see these scars and today His wounds testify of his victory. It is by these wounds we have been made whole (1 Pet. 2:24-25). When we learn how to be transparent with the pain that we have been through, our

scars become a testimony of the victories that God has given to us. Healing will flow to other people from the places, where we have been wounded the most. Where sin abounds, His grace will abound much more.

The grace of God is His active power in our lives and where we have been wounded by sin, or its consequences, we will also see the most powerful manifestations of His grace for restoration. When the Father restores, He always restores in abundance. He will not allow Satan to have the last word in any area of our lives. When we cooperate with the grace of God by giving Him access to our lives, we become a miracle in process.

Abraham Overcame His Failures

Abraham is a powerful example for us, as we walk in our calling. He never allowed his mistakes to define him, or to stop him from pursuing the vision of God. That is one of the major reasons that he became the father of our faith. We will sometimes fail and we will have long, hard battles with our weaknesses. Some of them, we might even have to struggle with for the rest of our lives, but that shouldn't be allowed to stop us. Our sins and failures have been crucified and reconciled in Christ, who has made all things new. As we give our failures and sins to the Father, He will use them to transform us into the image of Jesus. In the end, our story will become a testimony to the grace of God and the redeeming power of Jesus Christ.

Activations

- Abraham struggled with fear throughout his life, which caused him to make foolish decisions at times. Can you think of weaknesses in your life that keep reemerging in a similar way? How can these weaknesses be turned into portals for the grace and power of God? Take some time to process this with the Holy Spirit. Write down any new insight or strategy that you receive.

- Take some time to meditate on how the grace of God can redeem your pain, failures and weaknesses, so that they can become portals for the power of Christ. Read these scriptures together with the Holy Spirit:

    1. *Rom. 5:20-21*
    2. *2 Cor. 12:1-10*
    3. *2 Cor. 4:7-12*

  Pray and meditate upon these verses together with the Holy Spirit. Write down any insight and revelation that you receive.

- We learned this powerful Kingdom principle within this chapter: *Where sin abounded, His grace abounds much more!* Take 20- 30 minutes in prayer and ask the Father for His grace to abound in these three specific areas:

    1. *Your wounds.*
    2. *Your weaknesses and sins.*
    3. *Your mistakes and failures.*

  The Father wants to redeem your areas of pain and turn them into places of healing and restoration. Ask Him to make a crown of beauty out of your ashes.

- Ask the Father to take you on a journey into becoming a more authentic child of God. Ask Him to make you even more secure in His love, so that you can live an authentic life in all that you do.

CHAPTER 12: A GENEROUS HEART

Abraham and Sarah did not travel alone. In fact, they brought a whole company of people and animals with them. One of these people was Abraham's own nephew Lot. *"He took his wife, Sarai, his nephew Lot and all his wealth—his livestock and all the people he had taken into his household at Haran—and headed for the land of Canaan" (Gen. 12:5 NLT).* When they finally entered Canaan, even though it was peaceful among them at first, some challenges later emerged. These challenges put a strain on one of Abraham's key relationships.

Challenges will always arise as we possess the land that God has promised us. There will be battles that must be fought to take the promised land and there will be even more battles to fight if we want to possess and steward it. Abraham had to be reminded of this on several occasions. Sometimes, he handled his battles in an excellent way and sometimes, as we saw in the previous chapter, he failed. This gives us hope, because it shows us that Abraham was an ordinary human, just like us. As we walk with the Lord, we will go forth in victory, but sometimes that means that we're failing forward one step at a time. In this chapter, we are going to look at one specific challenge that arose, which Abraham dealt with in a way that sets a very good example for all of us.

A Lifestyle of Worship and Stewarding God's Blessings

Abraham was a blessed man full of God's favor, which had made him very rich. He was also a worshiper who loved God with all his heart. That's why he built altars everywhere.

(Abram was very rich in livestock, silver and gold.) From the Negev, they continued traveling by stages toward Bethel and they pitched their tents between Bethel and Ai, where they had camped before. This was

the same place where Abram had built the altar and there he worshiped the Lord again. (Gen. 13:2-4 NLT).

Loving God and living a lifestyle of worship, makes us safe for success. Our Father has never had any problem with us having a lot of money. He wants to give us a blessed life, but He does not want the money to have us. The problem is not in being rich, but the heart of the matter is always a matter of the heart. If we have a generous heart, wealth becomes a blessing. But if our hearts are greedy, wealth and money become an idol. We need to cultivate a lifestyle of worship and intimacy with Jesus. That will help us be good stewards of God's blessings.

The Challenge of Strife and Competition

Abraham's nephew, Lot, had become a wealthy man through his association with Abraham. If we spend time with people who are blessed and walk in the favor of God, that favor will rub off on us as well. That is one of the ways by which divine impartation works. This principle worked beautifully for Lot, but it caused a challenge. Almost all our important blessings and victories will bring its own challenges for us to deal with. The land was now no longer big enough for both of their flocks and herds. Since this caused serious strife between the herdsmen of Abraham and the people that worked for Lot, this became a quite serious problem. This is what happened:

Lot, who was traveling with Abram, had also become very wealthy with flocks of sheep and goats, herds of cattle and many tents. But the land could not support both Abram and Lot with all their flocks and herds living so close together. So disputes broke out between the herdsmen of Abram and Lot (Gen. 13:5-7 NLT).

When two blessed men with a huge vision must share space, the growth of these visions will sooner or later cause problems. Both

Abraham and Lot needed to expand their territories, because of the blessing of God. This really tested their hearts.

Knowing Whom to Bring with Us

This conflict broke out as a direct consequence of Abraham not paying attention to the instruction of God. *"Go from your country and from your relatives and from your father's house, to the land which I will show you"* (Gen. 12:1 NASB). Abraham had received crystal clear instructions from the Lord to leave his relatives behind, so it seems that he was making a mistake by even bringing Lot with him. As we move into our promised land and enter the Father's purpose for our lives, we need to be wise when it comes to whom we're bringing with us there. Those who want to join us in our vision must be called by the Lord. Otherwise, there will be a lot of conflict and unnecessary strife. Few things can ruin a person's heart as much as this type of strife. We must ask God for wisdom to pick the right people to be part of our team. As we are about to see, Abraham handled this situation in an extremely generous way. His actions revealed the heart of God.

Being Generous and Holding God's Promises with Open Hands

Abraham could have fought for his land by reminding Lot that God had given it to him as his inheritance. That would have been an understandable reaction. It would also have made this conflict worse and almost certainly have ruined Abraham's relationship with Lot. It would have opened a wide door for a spirit of strife and ambition to enter Abraham's heart and ministry. If a believer opens the door for that spirit, he will end up fighting in his own strength. Since the essence of faith is trusting in God, walking in strife and a competitive spirit is the opposite of faith. Abraham took the low road with God, by choosing to be generous instead. Faith always holds God's favor and promises with open hands.

So Abram said to Lot, "Please let there be no strife between you and me, nor between my herdsmen and your herdsmen, for we are relatives! Is the entire land not before you? Please separate from me; if you choose the left, then I will go to the right; or if you choose the right, then I will go to the left (Gen. 13:8-9 NASB).

Abraham didn't want to fight his own battles and neither was he interested in trying to fulfill God's promises in his own strength. Therefore, he gave Lot the opportunity to choose the part of the land that he liked the most. Abraham did not try to control God's plan. He knew that God had a plan ready to make all things turn out for our good (Rom. 8:28).

What God Has Given by Grace, Will Always Be Protected by His favor

We can learn a lot from this episode. We never need to succumb into trying to fulfill God's plan by our own strength and neither do we have to fight for our own rights in the Kingdom of God. When we allow God to fight for us, while at the same time living in generosity towards other people, we will always reap a greater harvest of blessings. We will always reap what we sow, but in a much greater measure.

Don't be misled: No one makes a fool of God. What a person plants, he will harvest. The person who plants selfishness, ignoring the needs of others—ignoring God!—harvests a crop of weeds. All he'll have to show for his life is weeds! But the one who plants in response to God, letting God's Spirit do the growth work in him, harvests a crop of real life, eternal life" (Gal. 6:7-8 The Message).

Therefore, we should take every chance we get to sow kindness and be generous. The principle of sowing and reaping will work for us, so that the life of Jesus can flow through us in even greater measures.

I have seen many precious believers lose their ministry and limit their calling, all because of strife and selfish ambitions. Strife is always rooted in fear and pride. Living in strife will take us down the road of compromise, where we will lose our integrity to gain influence by trying to control the Father's plans and purposes. There is no room for strife, church politics and selfish ambitions in the heart of a beloved child of God. We must humble ourselves and wait for the Father to open the right doors for us, in His own way and timing. We need to remember this principle: *What God has given by grace, will always be protected by His favor!* There is no need for us to be afraid to lose what God has given to us. He will fight our battles when we trust in Him.

Learning How to Lose Well

Lot made a very predictable choice. He chose the best part of the land, which contained the richest natural resources. In fact, it was such a rich land that it looked like the garden of the Lord (Gen. 13:10). *"So Lot chose for himself all the vicinity of the Jordan and Lot journeyed eastward. So they separated from each other" (Gen. 13:10-11 NASB).* Lot's selfish choice could have provoked Abraham in a big way. After all, giving Lot the opportunity to choose his part of the land first was very generous and Lot took full advantage of this offer. Abraham stood by his word and settled in the land of Canaan (Gen. 13:12). This shows us that Abraham had learned another important kingdom principle: *We always win with Jesus, by learning how to lose well.*

We need to learn the lesson of knowing how to lose well. When we give up our rights and claims, the Lord will fight our battles and make sure that His promises come to pass for us. Even if it looks like we are losing, God will be working for us to fulfill His promises. If we have been taken advantage of, or been bypassed, but manage to react with generosity and grace, we reflect the nature of Jesus. To walk in humility and generosity is more vital for us than having things going our way. God always resists the proud, but He gives grace to the humble (Jam. 4:6).

Selfish Motivation Brings a Snare

We saw earlier how acting out of selfish motivations will bring a harvest of corruption. In Lot's case, this was certainly true. Even if the part of the land which he chose was both beautiful and rich, its inhabitants were extremely wicked and ungodly. In fact, Lot moved to the worst possible place, by choosing to live so close to and later even in the city of Sodom itself. *"Abram settled in the land of Canaan, while Lot settled in the cities of the vicinity of the Jordan and moved his tents as far as Sodom. Now the men of Sodom were exceedingly wicked sinners against the Lord"* (Gen. 13:12-13 NASB).

A little earlier in this chapter, we noticed how divine impartation happens through association. Demonic impartation operates in a similar way. We sometimes underestimate the influence that the people we spend time with will have on our lives. In Lot's case, his carelessness in this area led to him living among people who had a very bad influence on him and his family. Lot had to live with the consequences of these bad choices for the rest of his life. Among these tragic consequences were losing his wife, nephews and that his daughters learned the immoral ways of Sodom (Gen. 19:14-38).

God Encourages Abraham by Reaffirming His Promises

Abraham gave up his rights to the best piece of the land to save his relationship with Lot. In the natural, it looked like he had lost God's promises by making this generous choice. However, when Abraham and Lot had gone their separate ways, God once again spoke encouraging words to confirm His powerful promises to Abraham: *"After Lot had gone, the Lord said to Abram, "Look as far as you can see in every direction—north and south, east and west. I am giving all this land, as far as you can see, to you and your descendants as a permanent possession" (Gen. 13:14-15 NLT).* There is so much power in possessing a spiritual vision. God knew that Abraham needed to remember his calling, so He gave a new picture to His friend by comparing the multiplication of his descendants to the dust of the earth. The Lord spoke about Abraham as a father of a people and revealed how fruitful he would become.

I will make your descendants as plentiful as the dust of the earth, so that if anyone can count the dust of the earth, then your descendants could also be counted. Arise, walk about in the land through its length and width; for I will give it to you (Gen. 13:14-18 NASB).

This promise gave strength and courage to Abraham! Our Father wants to comfort and encourage us during our spiritual battles and challenges. When we're building a vision and stewarding a call from God, we will face tough times where we must learn the lesson of losing well, just to survive spiritually. If that happens, it is very important that we know how to receive encouragement and comfort through our union with Jesus. We are one with Him and can drink from His love on a continual basis. Jesus Christ is the ultimate encourager. Comforting the believer is a big part of His present-day ministry. When we allow Him to minister to us, we are built up to take new territory for His kingdom.

Abraham Rescues Lot

Sometime after Lot had moved to Sodom, war broke out. Sodom was plundered and Lot was among the people, who were taken as prisoners of war. The hostile armies took his family, his goods and all his belongings. When Abraham heard that Lot had been captured, he gathered an army of his own to rescue him. He was successful in his rescue mission and not only did he recover all of Lot's family, but all his belongings as well (Gen. 14:1-17). This reveals something important about Abraham. He held no grudge at all against Lot. He wanted Lot to be both safe and blessed!

A big part of knowing how to lose well is found in learning how to keep our hearts pure. We need to love mercy and actively pray for those who has taken advantage of us. The Lord wants us to find ways to support and pray for them. That is Christlikeness in action!

Abraham Meets Melchizedek

After Abraham returned from the battlefield an interesting man by the name of Melchizedek brought a meal, consisting of bread and wine to Abraham. Melchizedek was the king of Salem and a priest of God.

And Melchizedek, the king of Salem and a priest of God Most High, brought Abram some bread and wine. Melchizedek blessed Abram with this blessing: "Blessed be Abram by God Most High, Creator of heaven and earth. And blessed be God Most High, who has defeated your enemies for you" (Gen. 14:18-20 NLT).

It is obvious that Melchizedek is a type of Jesus Christ, or maybe even Jesus Himself, appearing in His pre-incarnate form. Since I wrote a whole chapter on Melchizedek in a previous book, I will just mention his encounter with Abraham briefly here (see my book *The burning love of Jesus Christ*). Whether we believe that he is Jesus appearing in the Old Testament or not, we can all agree that Melchizedek is probably the most obvious picture of Jesus in the Old Testament. This is how Melchizedek is a type of Christ:

- *He is a priest, a king and a prophet (Hebr. 7:1).*
- *He is the king of righteousness and the king of peace (Hebr. 7:2).*
- *He blessed God's chosen one and celebrated his victory with a meal, serving bread and wine (Gen. 14:18).*
- *He is without beginning of days or end of life (Hebr. 7:3).*
- *He remains a priest forever (Hebr.7:3).*

- *He is not a descendant of Levi but has become a priest based on an indestructible life (Hebr. 7:6, 16-17).*
- *He is greater than Abraham (Hebr. 7:6-7).*

The similarities between Jesus and Melchizedek are too many to be coincidental. This king made a strong impression on Abraham who gave him a tenth of everything that he had recovered from the battle. *"Then Abram gave Melchizedek a tenth of all the goods he had recovered" (Gen. 14:18-20 NLT).*

Abraham and the King of Sodom

After Abraham had met Melchizedek, the king of Sodom showed up to congratulate Abraham and he came to present a generous offer. *"The king of Sodom said to Abram, "Give back my people who were captured. But you may keep for yourself all the goods you have recovered" (Rev. 14.21 NLT).* This was a way for the king of Sodom to show his gratefulness. After all, Abraham had rescued most of the inhabitants of Sodom that had been captured during the war. He did the king of Sodom a huge favor by doing that. However, Abraham gave a very firm response to this grateful king.

Abram replied to the king of Sodom, "I solemnly swear to the Lord, God Most High, Creator of heaven and earth, that I will not take so much as a single thread or sandal thong from what belongs to you. Otherwise you might say, 'I am the one who made Abram rich (Gen. 14:22-23 NLT).

The reason that Abraham responded like this, was that he knew about the principle of spiritual impartation. The king of Sodom was an ungodly man and Abraham didn't want to be associated with him at all. This is a very different way of thinking compared to that of Lot. Lot was mostly interested in the wealth of the land, to the point that he ignored the way that Sodom were corrupting his life. Abraham on the other hand, was much more interested in a pure heart than in material wealth and worldly possessions.

Consequently, he rejected the king's generous offer. This saying of Jesus comes to mind here: *"What bliss you experience when your heart is pure! For then your eyes will open to see more and more of God" (Matt. 5:8 TPT).* To have an ever-expanding revelation of the Father's heart is much more precious, than all the wealth and blessings that this world can offer to us!

We can learn many lessons, by observing how Abraham handled the king of Sodom here. One such lesson would be learning this very basic, but still very important Kingdom principle: *Spiritual impartation always happens through association.* The kind of people we that we chose to associate with, will always impart whatever they carry in their hearts into our lives. It is important that we're receiving the pure life of Jesus from the people that we keep the closest to us. Wealth, significance and shortsighted benefits are never more important than a pure heart and integrity. Our Father has promised to provide all our needs and we need to trust Him to do that.

Activations

- In this chapter, we have studied Abraham's generosity and kindness toward Lot. Read the whole story in prayer together with Jesus. You'll find it in Gen. 13:1-14:17. What lessons do you learn by studying this story? How does it benefit your life with Jesus to walk in generosity? Invite the Holy Spirit to reveal more insights to you from this story. Write down any insights that you get.

- Take some time to reflect and meditate on the following Kingdom principles that we found in this chapter. Invite the Holy Spirit to speak to you through them:

    1. *We win with Jesus, by learning how to lose well.*
    2. *What God has given by grace, will always be protected by His favor.*
    3. *Spiritual impartation happens through association.*

    How can living by these principles benefit your life and ministry? Have you applied them in your life? Pray over them and write down any revelation or insight that you receive.

- Take 20-30 minutes in prayer to ask the Father to fill you with a generous spirit and an anointing for giving. Repent from any strife or competition that have entered your life. Ask the Father to purify your life from all strife and competition.

- Take time to pray and intercede for the body of Christ. Ask the Father to baptize us in generosity and to deliver the body of Christ from all strongholds of strife and the competitive spirit.

CHAPTER 13: THE LORD'S COVENANT

PARTNER

We have already quoted the promises that God gave to Abraham concerning the blessings upon his offspring and children, several times throughout this book. These promises were unconditional, purely based on the goodness and grace of God and they are the foundation for the Abrahamic covenant, which we will study in this chapter. This is what God promised Abraham:

Get out of your country, from your family and from your father's house, to a land that I will show you. I will make you a great nation; I will bless you and make your name great; and you shall be a blessing. I will bless those who bless you and I will curse him who curses you; and in you all the families of the earth shall be blessed (Gen. 12:1-3 NKJV).

In this chapter, we will study the events that took place when the Lord confirmed His promise to Abraham by entering a covenant with him. Jesus is the final fulfillment of the Abrahamic covenant and through Him, we have been made the rightful heirs to all the promises and blessings of Abraham. This makes it important for us to gain a deeper understanding of the Abrahamic covenant.

The Lord revealed Himself to Abraham in a vision to assure him that there was no need to fear. The Lord Himself promised to be Abraham's shield of protection, who would reward him greatly. Our Father loves to reward His people. *"After these things the word of the Lord came to Abram in a vision, saying, "Do not fear, Abram, I am a shield to you; Your reward shall be very great" (Gen. 15:1 NASB).* Abraham wrestled with questions concerning how this could be possible, since he had no heir. He shared this concern with God, who reassured Abraham that he would be blessed with a son.

God promised to give Canaan to the descendants of Abraham as an inheritance. His descendants would become more numerous than the stars in the sky. Abraham was going to become fruitful and multiply (Gen. 15:2-7).

Processing Doubts and Questions

Even though Abraham had received all these powerful promises from the Lord, he still had a hard time believing God. Abraham was still questioning if God could keep His promises (Gen. 15:8). Since the fulfillment of these promises required a huge miracle, his reaction was understandable. The doubts and questions that Abraham struggled with was no problem for God. He made the right choice by processing his doubts with the Lord. This is true in our case as well. When we process our doubts with God, they become a pathway to greater faith. Jesus is not nervous or shaken by our doubts, but He wants to be involved in them. We involve Him by surrendering our doubts to Him and by choosing to trust Him anyway. That always opens the door to greater faith.

The Covenant That Secures the Promises

The Lord did something very radical to reassure Abraham about the fulfilment of the promises. God spoke to Abraham:

Bring Me a three-year-old heifer, a three-year-old female goat, a three-year-old ram, a turtledove and a young pigeon." Then he brought all these to Him and cut them in two, down the middle and placed each piece opposite the other; but he did not cut the birds in two (Gen 15:8-10 NKJV).

God wanted to make a covenant with Abraham. It might be hard for us to understand the significance of what God did here, but for Abraham this was mind-blowing. In that time and culture, cutting a covenant was common practice. For example, we later learn how Abraham himself entered a covenant with Abimelech

(Gen. 21:22-34). Cutting a covenant was a serious matter during this time. The two parties that entered into the covenant with one another, were bound to honor it unto death. When the Lord told Abraham to bring the animals and cut them in pieces, he knew that whatever God had promised would come to pass. To break the covenant was to lose all honor and it was considered as a very shameful act in that culture. He knew that the Lord would never break His own covenant!

The Slavery in Egypt Is Foretold

Then Abraham fell asleep and the Lord came to him in a dream. He revealed that Abraham's descendants were going to live in another country where they would be enslaved. *"You can be sure that your descendants will be strangers in a foreign land, where they will be oppressed as slaves for 400 years. But I will punish the nation that enslaves them and in the end they will come away with great wealth" (Gen. 15:13-14 NLT).* This needed to happen for the sins of the Amorites, who inhabited Canaan during that time to reach its full measure. When that had happened, they would be driven out and Abraham's descendants would finally fully possess their promised land. *"After four generations your descendants will return here to this land, for the sins of the Amorites do not yet warrant their destruction" (Gen. 15:16 NLT).* It is impressive that Abraham had such a long-term vision. God had given this land to him and yet these promises would manifest fully hundreds of years later. In his brilliant defense speech before the council, Stephen had this to say about Abraham: *"But He gave him no inheritance in it, not even a foot of ground and yet, He promised that He would give it to him as a possession and to his descendants after him, even though he had no child" (Acts 7:5 NASB).* This sets a good example for us. We often have a very short-term way of looking at the promises of God, thinking that they should manifest immediately, but it is through patience and faith that we inherit the promises. We always live in the tension of already, but not yet, in the Kingdom of God.

The Covenant Is Established

The Lord then initiated the ritual that was usually performed as two parties entered a covenant. *"Now it came about, when the sun had set, that it was very dark and behold, a smoking oven and a flaming torch appeared which passed between these pieces. On that day the Lord made a covenant with Abram"* (Gen. 15:17-18 NASB). But already here, we find a clue that something was going to be different with this covenant. Usually, both covenant partners had to partake in the ritual by walking between the pieces of animals, but this was not a covenant between two equal parties. God put Abraham to sleep to show him that this would be an unconditional covenant. Therefore, only the Lord passed between the pieces of animals. He was the only one making promises within this covenant. This covenant was based on the grace and goodness of God alone. Abraham's part was to receive it by faith!

A Flaming Torch

When the Lord passed between the pieces of animals to confirm the covenant, He appeared in the shape of a flaming torch. This is significant. The flaming torch was a prophetic picture that was meant as a revelation of the Lord's burning love for His people. The love of the Lord is described as a flame of fire that cannot be quenched, all throughout the scriptures (Song. 8:6-7). The Lord of love entered a covenant with Abraham, purely based on His own goodness and grace. This is who our heavenly Father is and that will always be His heart towards us. He always relates to us in love, goodness and grace!

The Promise of the Covenant

The Lord confirmed that He had given the promised land to the descendants of Abraham. *"So the Lord made a covenant with Abram that day and said, "I have given this land to your descendants, all the way from the border of Egypt to the great Euphrates River (Gen. 15:18-*

20 NLT). Since this promise was given without conditions, it was based on the grace and goodness of God. When the Lord entered the covenant with Abraham, Abraham became fully convinced that he was going to be the father of a great nation and people. The Lord has always been a God of covenants and the covenants that He has entered with His people, has always been His way to let us know that He keeps His promises. Abraham was now the Lord's covenant partner.

The Five Biblical Covenants

Within the Scriptures, we can find five covenants. It is important to know the difference between these. When we understand the different covenants, the Bible makes sense and it becomes much easier to understand God's actions. Otherwise, some of God's acts will be very hard to understand and they may even appear to contradict His nature as revealed in Jesus Christ. But once we understand that God relates and acts towards His people based on covenants, we'll get a clearer picture of the reason behind His actions. The five covenants in the Bible are:

1. *The Noahic Covenant*
    God's covenant with Noah was an unconditional type of covenant, in which the Lord promised never to destroy the earth through a flood again. Noah had no active part to play in this covenant. It was built on God's promises. *"I establish My covenant with you; and all flesh shall never again be eliminated by the waters of a flood, nor shall there again be a flood to destroy the earth" (Gen. 9:11 NASB)*. As a sign that this covenant would remain forever, the Lord put the rainbow in the sky (Gen. 9:12-13).

2. *The Abrahamic Covenant*
    God's covenant with Abraham, which we are focusing on in this chapter, was an unconditional covenant. It was built only on the Lord's promises to bless him and make

his offspring into a blessing for the whole world. In this chapter, we're studying how God enacted this covenant, but the promises it rested upon were given to Abraham long before it had been enacted. *"And I will make you into a great nation and I will bless you and make your name great; and you shall be a blessing; and I will bless those who bless you and the one who curses you I will curse. And in you all the families of the earth will be blessed"* (Gen. 12:2-3 NASB). These were unconditional promises of God to Abraham, purely based on His goodness and grace!

3. ***The Mosaic/Old Covenant***
    God wanted to establish an unconditional covenant with the people of Israel as well, where they would all be His priests, but they rejected that. Instead, they chose Moses as their mediator and opted for a conditional covenant. The old covenant doesn't reflect the relationship that the Lord wanted with His people, but the relationship that they wanted with God (Exod. 19-20, Deut. 5).

4. ***The Davidic Covenant***
    This was also an unconditional covenant, built purely on the grace and goodness of God. God promised to build a house to David and that one of his descendants would rule his kingdom forever. *"The Lord also declares to you that the Lord will make a house for you. When your days are finished and you lie down with your fathers, I will raise up your descendant after you, who will come from you and I will establish his kingdom. He shall build a house for My name and I will establish the throne of his kingdom forever (2 Sam 7:11-12 NASB).* These promises referred partly to Solomon, David's son and heir in the natural. However, their true and final fulfillment took place through Jesus, who now reigns forever, sitting on the throne of David, which is why the Lord proclaimed to David: *"Your house and your*

kingdom shall endure before Me forever; your throne shall be established forever" (2 Sam. 7:16 NASB).

5. ***The New Covenant***
   The New Covenant was established by Jesus through the cross. The New Covenant fulfills the Abrahamic and the Davidic covenants, while at the same time removing the old covenant forever. It is for this reason that we are now totally delivered from the law and have inherited the full blessing of Abraham. The New Covenant is built on the grace of God alone. It is an unconditional covenant.

We Have a Better Covenant

Like Abraham, we are God's covenant partners today. In fact, we have a much better covenant, which is called the New Covenant. In the book of Hebrews, the New Covenant is even called a better covenant. *"But now He has obtained a more excellent ministry, to the extent that He is also the mediator of a better covenant, which has been enacted on better promises"* (Hebr. 8:6 NASB). In previous books, I have already written several chapters, describing life in the New Covenant, so I will not repeat that teaching here (See my books *The Burning Love of Jesus Christ & Transformed by the Grace of God*). But it is very important for us to be fully rooted and established within the realities of the New Covenant to fully take advantage of all its benefits and blessings. The old covenant passed away a long time ago and it is time for us to leave it behind. Let us fully embrace the New Covenant with its superior promises instead. In the book of Hebrews, we find several New Covenant blessings that will help us break new ground for the Kingdom of God:

- *We are holy and perfected in Christ (Hebr. 10:10,14)*
- *The Father has promised to never remember our sins and iniquities (Hebr. 8:12, 10:17-18)*
- *His will is written in our hearts (Hebr. 8:10, 10:16)*

- *We have a corporate identity as His people and family (Hebr. 8:10)*
- *We know the Father (Hebr. 8:11)*

These are very simple and profound truths of the New Covenant. They give us boldness and confidence to move forward with the vision that God has given to us. For example, knowing that Jesus will never remember our sins and that He has made us holy and perfect sets us free from sin consciousness. It delivers us from the need for constant self-evaluation, so that we can focus on the will of God.

Circumcision as a Sign

Later, when the Lord reminded Abraham of the promises He had given, He revealed what the sign of His covenant with Abraham was going to be: *"This is My covenant which you shall keep, between Me and you and your descendants after you: Every male child among you shall be circumcised; and you shall be circumcised in the flesh of your foreskins and it shall be a sign of the covenant between Me and you" (Gen. 17:10-11 NASB).* Circumcision was a serious matter to God back then. In fact, He commanded that if any uncircumcised males were found among them, they were to be executed (Gen. 17:14). Circumcision was a very important identity marker, given to remind God's chosen people that they were in covenant with Him. Stephen even refers to God's covenant with Abraham as a covenant of circumcision (Acts 7:8). It was while the Lord spoke to Abraham about circumcision that He changed his name. We will look at the significance of that later in this book.

Circumcision of the Heart

Circumcision was an act of prophetic symbolism, which spoke of the cutting away of the old man. Paul wrote on the circumcision of the heart in Romans: *"For he is not a Jew who is one outwardly, nor is circumcision that which is outward in the flesh. But he is a Jew who is one inwardly; and circumcision is of the heart, by the Spirit, not by the letter; and his praise is not from people, but from God"* (Rom. 2:28-29 NASB). In the New Covenant, our identity markers aren't outward signs or rituals. We no longer need to keep the Sabbath, or the food regulations of the old covenant. Neither do we need to circumcise people who are born again. In the New Covenant, circumcision is a work of the Holy Spirit within the heart of the believer, which delivers us from our old life. This work has been done through the cross.

For if we have become united with Him in the likeness of His death, certainly we shall also be in the likeness of His resurrection, knowing this, that our old self was crucified with Him, in order that our body of sin might be done away with, so that we would no longer be slaves to sin (Rom. 6:5-6 NASB).

Our hearts have already been circumcised and we have died to our old life. We apply this reality in the New Covenant by simply surrendering our bodies to Christ, so that He can live through us. We are reconciled through the death of Jesus, but we are saved by His life (Rom. 6:11-14, Gal. 2:19-21). By depending on Jesus to live His life through us, we can walk in holiness and put off the old man. We have been commanded to *"… to put off your old self, which is being corrupted by its deceitful desires; to be made new in the attitude of your minds; and to put on the new self, created to be like God in true righteousness and holiness"* (Eph. 4:22-24 NIV). This can only be done by allowing Jesus to express His life and nature through us. To be fully delivered from our old life is one of the greatest blessings of the New Covenant. We are set free to put on the new man so that we can live in newness of life. We can live in constant renewal with Jesus and break through into new areas in the spirit to extend the Kingdom of God.

Every Promise Is Yes and Amen in Christ

As we have already seen, the Father is extremely serious when it comes to His covenants. He has guaranteed to fulfil His promises to us, because all His promises are sealed by the blood of Christ. *"For all the promises of God in Him are Yes and in Him Amen, to the glory of God through us" (2 Cor. 1:20 NKJV).* Every promise in the Bible, as well as all the promises that Jesus have spoken to us personally, are yes and amen in Christ. We can boldly build our vision, knowing that our Father will keep His promises and that He will always do what He told us. This is the power of the New Covenant. It gives us boldness and freedom because we can rest in all His promises.

Promises of Fruitfulness and Breakthrough

Since we live in the New Covenant, every promise in the Bible now belongs to us. His Word is packed with wonderful promises that will help us build a fruitful vision, while at the same time living meaningful and satisfying lives with Jesus. All the Father's promises now belong to us and they have become our birthright. I love to declare the promises of God over my life. This has been a very life-giving and empowering habit for me in my walk with God. All His promises are yes and amen for us in Christ. We can walk in full assurance and confidence that they will be fulfilled.

We can use His promises as declarations to encourage ourselves in the Lord. They are a tool to establish ourselves in our identity as the Father's beloved, fruitful and favored child. Since we are His children and heirs, these promises are our birthright through Christ. I recommend that you make your own list of declarations, based on biblical promises. Declaring the Word of God releases His power to work on your behalf. It will also help us keep our focus on His promises. Let's follow Abraham's example in this, by placing our full assurance and confidence in the promises of God and the New Covenant!

Activations

- Just like the Abrahamic covenant, the New Covenant is unconditional, purely based on the goodness and grace of God. How does that benefit your relationship with the Father? How can it help your ministry to know that your work is built on grace alone? Process and pray over this truth together with the Holy Spirit.

- The book of Hebrews paints a clear and beautiful picture of the New Covenant, especially chapter 8-11. Read and study these chapters to find more revelation on the New Covenant. Invite the Holy Spirit to give more insight to you on the New Covenant. Write down the insights that you find.

- We have seen how all the promises of God belong to us in the New Covenant. I have picked a few promises from the Scriptures and made a list of biblical declarations to illustrate how to speak and proclaim the Word of God:

1. *The world is my inheritance (Rom. 4:13).*
2. *I'm chosen by Jesus Himself to glorify my heavenly Father by bearing much lasting fruit (John 15:16).*
3. *I am planted in the love of Christ and whatever I set my hands to, will prosper (Ps. 1:3).*
4. *I ask for the nations and the are given to me as my inheritance (Ps. 2:8).*
5. *I'm rising up to shine, because my light has come and the glory of the Lord has risen upon me (Isa. 60:1).*
6. *The Lord increases and renews my strength, so that I can carry the vision without growing weary (Isa. 40:29-30).*

Find at least ten more promises in the Bible and use them to make your own declarations. Then ask the Holy Spirit to highlight some more biblical promises that He wants you to use as prophetic declarations. Write them down.

- Take 20-30 minutes in prayer. Meditate, proclaim, speak and pray these declarations over your life, ministry and family. This will release the power of Christ to work for you. Keep on doing this regularly.

- Take some time in prayer and intercession for the body of Christ. Ask the Father to unveil the New Covenant in a deeper way to us. Ask Him to take us deeper into new creation realities.

CHAPTER 14: IDENTITY AND FRUITFULNESS

Abraham and Sarah didn't just receive the promise to inherit a nation, but God promised to bless them with a child as well. God had promised Abraham to multiply his offspring and make them a whole new people and a great nation (Gen. 13:14-17, 15:4-5). Since both were long past childbearing age, the fulfillment of this promise required a big miracle, but we know that our Father is a specialist when it comes to big miracles. Miracles from God often release a much greater blessing than we would have ever been able to dream or even think of (Eph. 3:20-21).

We know that God did heal Sarah from barrenness and enabled her to have a child and heir. *"And by faith even Sarah, who was past childbearing age, was enabled to bear children because she considered him faithful who had made the promise" (Hebr.11:11 NIV).* Not only did Abraham and Sarah have a son in the natural. They became the spiritual parents of all of God's children as well, which means that they have been blessed with countless descendants, of both natural and spiritual descent. *"And so from this one man and he as good as dead, came descendants as numerous as the stars in the sky and as countless as the sand on the seashore" (Hebr. 11:12 NIV).* However, before Abraham and Sarah could become parents, they needed a renewed revelation of their identity. Since Sarai had been barren for so long, she had made the shame and pain of barrenness into her identity. *"But Sarai was barren; she had no child" (Gen. 11:30).* This had become a big stronghold that needed to be broken. God started to break these lies by revealing their true identity, as he changed their names.

A New Name – a New Identity

At the time when Abraham was called by the Lord to leave his land, as well as throughout their journey to Canaan, their names were still Abram and Sarai. But sometime after they had settled in the land, God changed their name to Abraham and Sarah. This was a significant moment. Their identity began to shift when the Lord changed their names. The reason for that becomes obvious when we understand the meaning of their new names:

- **Abram** means *"exalted father"*. Abraham means *"father of multitudes"*.
- **Sarai** means *princess.* Sarah has a similar meaning, but the changing of her name speaks of upgraded identity, fruitfulness and renewal. Both Paul and Isaiah confirm this by referring to Sarah as our mother (Isa. 51:2-3, Gal. 4:21-31).

Their names became a prophetic declaration of their calling to be parents of a new people and nation, as well as the parents of our faith. In the Scriptures, a name given by God will almost always carries prophetic significance. God never gave people their name randomly. The Lord always gave new names as a declaration to reveal prophetic identity and calling, which pointed to a person's future in God.

We Have Received a New Name

We'll find a powerful example of this in the book of Revelation. In the letters to the seven churches, Jesus gives some wonderful promises to the overcoming believers (For more on this topic, see my book *The Burning Love of Jesus Christ*). To the church located in the city of Pergamum, Jesus gives this promise about receiving a new name. *"The one who has an ear, let him hear what the Spirit says to the churches. To the one who overcomes, I will give some of the hidden manna and I will give him a white stone and a new name written on the stone which no one knows except the one who receives it"* (Rev. 2:17 NASB). One of the benefits of being in Christ is that we now have received a new name. Just like Abraham and Sarah, this name is meant to be a prophetic declaration of our new identity.

Our corporate identity is only found in Christ. That is our family name, but we also have a personal identity. Our personal identity in Christ, consists of our personality, our purpose, as well as our gifts and calling. This is the reason that He has given us our new name.

Identity and Fulfilled Promises

We can learn an important principle here. At this point, Abraham had already received the promise of having a child and he knew that his offspring would multiply and become a new nation. This had already been fully established through his covenant with the Lord. Abraham was certain that this was going to happen and he had already been justified by his faith. *"And he brought him forth abroad and said, Look now toward heaven and tell the stars, if thou be able to number them: and he said unto him, So shall thy seed be. And he believed in the LORD; and he counted it to him for righteousness"* *(Gen. 15:5-6).* However, a very important piece of the puzzle was still missing in his life. Before the promises of God could manifest fully for Abraham and Sarah, they had to get a revelation of their real identity in God. This is a Kingdom principle that we can find all throughout the Bible: *A revelation of our identity in Christ brings manifestation of the Father's promises.*

The promises of God are powerful enough to transform our lives, but for that to happen, we need to be set free from the devil's lies of who we are. Receiving God's promises while still living from our old identity limits their fulfillment in our lives. For God's will to prosper and be fruitful, we need to walk in a revelation of who we are in Christ. I have seen how this principle works in my own life on several occasions. Every time that God starts to bring me into a greater fulfillment of His plan for my life, He always begin by giving me a deeper revelation of my identity in Christ.

An Upgraded Identity

Before Abraham and Sarah could fulfill their calling to be a father and mother of a new people, they needed a huge upgrade in their revelation of their identity. God changed their names to make a prophetic declaration of fruitfulness over them. They had been barren and had carried that as a spiritual identity and a mark of shame. God spoke destiny into their life by changing their names and declaring who they really were in His eyes. He changed their names to reveal their calling. First, God spoke to Abraham: *"No longer shall you be named Abram, but your name shall be Abraham; For I have made you the father of a multitude of nations. I will make you exceedingly fruitful and I will make nations of you and kings will come from you (Gen. 17:4-6 NASB).* Then God continued to speak to Abraham and told him that circumcision would be the sign of their covenant (Gen. 17:9-14). Finally, the Lord revealed the new name and identity of Sarai as well: *"As for your wife Sarai, you shall not call her by the name Sarai, but Sarah shall be her name. I will bless her and indeed I will give you a son by her. Then I will bless her and she shall be a mother of nations; kings of peoples will come from her (Gen. 17:15-16 NASB).* It is significant that Abraham and Sarah's names were changed, while the Lord spoke about the covenant.

A new identity and a fruitful life are connected to our covenant with God. He has promised both to restore our identity and that we will bear a lot of lasting fruit! This change of identity did not happen at the start of their journey with the Lord, but it needed to happen at some point in their walk with God. Right from the moment that God changed their names, they went by their new names, Abraham and Sarah. This means that every time someone called them by their new name, it became a powerful reminder and declaration of their identity and destiny.

Embracing Our New Identity

When Abraham and Sarah embraced their new names, it meant that they embraced an identity of blessing and fruitfulness. Their past could no longer define them. Instead, they allowed the Lord to define them, so that their future could be shaped by their new identity as His chosen ones. This same principle applies to us. We are now living in the New Covenant. Knowing who we are as children of God is foundational for everything else in our life with Jesus. We need a deeper revelation of our corporate identity as the Father's family, as well as knowing our personal identity in Christ.

Our Father wants us to embrace our new identity and live out of the inheritance that He has given to us. *"Look with wonder at the depth of the Father's marvelous love that he has lavished on us! He has called us and made us his very own beloved children. The reason the world doesn't recognize who we are is that they didn't recognize him"* (*1 John 3:1 TPT*). We are His children and He generously lavishes His love upon us. Knowing who we are in Christ, establishes us in our corporate identity as His children, but the Father desires a personal relationship with each one of His children. Therefore, He has given each one of us a new individual identity as well. As we saw earlier in this chapter, our individual identity in Christ, consists of our personality, our gifts and the purpose for which God created us. He calls each one of us by a new name!

Three Perspectives on Identity

The Bible shows us three different perspectives of identity, which come from very different sources. It is important to know about these perspectives, so that we can discern which influences we're allowing to define us. I have written on these three perspectives in previous books (*Abiding in the Father's Love* & *The Burning Love of Jesus Christ*). However, I want to mention them again for a very simple reason. Abraham and Sarah's journey into their prophetic identity is a journey of transition through these perspectives. We are now going to look at their journey to draw some insights that will help us in our own journey as well:

1.   *Satan's Perspective on Identity - Our Broken Past*

Since Satan is the accuser of the brethren and a lying deceiver, he uses past sins, failures and wounds to define who we are and to stamp a fallen identity upon us. According to him, we are forever defined by our broken and sinful past (Rev. 12:9-10). In the case of Abraham and Sarah, this meant that they were forever stuck in barrenness and unfruitfulness. When we first read about them, they had accepted Satan's view of their lives. Consequently, they viewed themselves as barren and unfruitful. They were trapped in the shame and pain of their past, which gave Satan the power to oppress them with lies and false accusations. In our case, there are other issues from the past that Satan uses to define us, but the principle will always remain the same. If we buy into Satan's lies of our lives, we will be bound by our past sins and brokenness.

2.   *The Human Perspective on Identity - Present Circumstances*

Man defines one another according to the flesh, which means by natural knowledge (2 Cor. 5:16). While Satan uses our *broken past* to define us, people will use *present circumstances* to define who we are and measure our capacity for God. Present circumstances would include things like our career, education and our social status. According to this perspective, we are defined by where we are in life right now. For Abraham and Sarah, this would have meant remaining childless, without an heir. Even if they would have been healed from the shame of barrenness, they would still have been unable to have a child. This would have meant being trapped within the limits of what seemed humanly possible.

Sarah viewed herself in this way when she heard of the exciting news that God spoke to Abraham concerning the birth of Isaac: *"Then one of them said, "I will return to you about this time next year and your wife, Sarah, will have a son!" Sarah was listening to this conversation from the tent (Gen. 18:10 NLT).* She overheard how the Lord told Abraham that the time when they would receive their promised child was coming closer, but while she was listening, she fell back into her old fallen thought patterns again. *"Abraham and Sarah were both very old by this time and Sarah was long past the age of having children. So she laughed silently to herself and said, "How could a worn-out woman like me enjoy such pleasure, especially when my master—my husband—is also so old" (Gen. 18:11-12 NLT).* This is a good illustration of how the human perspective affects our identity in a way that limits us in a dramatic way. In the natural, it was impossible for Abraham and Sarah to have a child, but the Lord is never limited by our circumstances. When we're walking together with Him, all things are possible!

3.   *The Father's Perspective on Identity - In Christ and Our Prophetic Future*

When God looks at us, He sees us in Christ and who we are about to become (2 Cor. 5:17). So, while Satan will use our *past* to define us and humans views us through our *present* circumstances, God sees us according to our *prophetic future*. He sees the person that we are becoming. According to His perspective, our identity is defined by who we are in Christ and who we will be when the transforming work of Jesus is finished. In other words, the Father sees the finished product of our lives. This is what He wanted to communicate by changing Abraham and Sarah's names. From the Lord's perspective, Abraham was already a father of nations and Sarah was a fruitful princess. As they embraced their names, they started to become rooted in their new identity.

Sarah Laughed

For this reason, the Lord had to address Sarah's laughter and her unbelief. The Lord didn't rebuke her to shame her, but He called her out to bring her back into faith. *"Then the Lord said to Abraham, "Why did Sarah laugh? Why did she say, 'Can an old woman like me have a baby?' Is anything too hard for the Lord? I will return about this time next year and Sarah will have a son" (Gen. 18:13-14 NLT).* When Sarah realized that her laughter of unbelief had been exposed, it rattled her and she became a little nervous. *"Sarah was afraid, so she denied it, saying, "I didn't laugh." But the Lord said, "No, you did laugh" (Gen. 18:15 NLT).* When our shortcomings are exposed, we need to remember that Jesus is our friend. With a smile the Lord reminded Sarah that He knew that she had laughed. He needed to do this to set her free from unbelief and from her own human perspective. God did this as an act of grace because the way He saw it, Abraham and Sarah were a fruitful and blessed couple!

Isaac Is Born

Our Father is full of grace and faithfulness. He kept His promise and within a year Sarah gave birth to a son.

The Lord graciously remembered and visited Sarah as He had said and the Lord did for her as He had promised. So Sarah conceived and gave birth to a son for Abraham in his old age, at the appointed time of which God had spoken to him. Abraham named his son Isaac (laughter), the son to whom Sarah gave birth (Gen. 21:1-3 AMP).

When Abraham and Sarah stepped into their prophetic destiny in God, the promise of a son became reality. They already were a blessed and fruitful couple. Finally, their present circumstances matched that reality. This is how revelation of identity proceeds the fulfilment of God's promises and it is an important spiritual principle that applies to all of God's people. This miracle not only gave them a child. The Lord healed Sarah from the shame of her barrenness as well. Her joy was restored and even though Sarah had laughed at the promises of God, the Lord got the last laugh! *"Sarah said, 'God has made me laugh; all who hear [about our good news] will laugh with me.' And she said, 'Who would have said to Abraham that Sarah would nurse children? For I have given birth to a son by him in his old age'"* (Gen. 21:6-7 AMP). We can always count on God's goodness and grace to work for us. He loves us and He will always keep His promises! He will not always fulfill them in the way we expected, but He will always do what He said. Jesus is faithful and in Him, all the Father's promises belong to us.

Revelation of Identity and Faith in God's Promise

We can see how Abraham now had become firmly established in his God-given identity by reading the following scripture:

Even when there was no reason for hope, Abraham kept hoping—believing that he would become the father of many nations. For God had said to him, "That's how many descendants you will have! "And Abraham's faith did not weaken, even though, at about 100 years of age, he figured his body was as good as dead—and so was Sarah's womb" (Rom. 4:18-19 NLT).

The devil probably told Abraham that it was already too late for a miracle and that they had been doomed to a life of barrenness and shame. His friends and family were telling him that this was impossible and that they should stop trying to deny reality, but Abraham no longer paid attention to these voices. He listened to what God said and God promised to bless Abraham and Sarah with many descendants. Abraham fully embraced this promise of fruitfulness and trusted in what God had said. *"Abraham never wavered in believing God's promise. In fact, his faith grew stronger and in this he brought glory to God. He was fully convinced that God is able to do whatever he promises"* (Rom. 4:20-21 NLT). Walking in an increasing revelation of our identity in Christ and having faith in

God's promises, will release a full manifestation of God's will in our lives.

This is one of the most important lessons that the Father taught me, when I embraced the calling that He had given to me. To live and operate out of my identity as His beloved and favored son, creates the kind of faith in His goodness and grace that brings all God's promises into reality.

<h1 style="text-align:center">Activations</h1>

- In this chapter, we have studied how Abraham and Sarah received new names and how that transformed their identity. Find three more examples where names carry prophetic significance in the Bible. Study these three examples to learn more about identity. How did a new name change their lives? Why were their names significant? Write down any insight that you receive.

- We saw how the Bible describes three perspectives on identity, coming from different sources:

  1. *Satan's Perspective - Your Broken Past.*
  2. *Man's Perspective - Your Present Circumstances.*
  3. *The Father's Perspective - In Christ and Prophetic Future*

  Make three different identity statements that are based on each one of these perspectives. How does the devil look at you? What is man's perspective of you? How does the Father look at you? Write an identity statement on each of these perspectives.

- Take 20-30 minutes in prayer. Break the perspectives of Satan and man off your life. If you discern that there are still areas in your life where you have agreed with Satan or man's perspective, repent and invite Jesus to reveal who you really are in these areas. Tear apart or delete the identity statements based on the two fallen perspectives from the previous activation. Invite the Holy Spirit to take you deeper into the Father's view of who you are.

- We have received a new name in Christ. This is clearly revealed in Rev. 2:17. Read and process this verse with Jesus. Ask Him to reveal your new name and how this name reflects your identity and purpose. Write down your new name and what it reveals about you.

CHAPTER 15: WE ARE CHILDREN OF THE FREE WOMAN

In Galatians, Paul refers to Sarah as an allegorical picture of the New Covenant. Sarah is the free woman, who gives birth to her offspring through the power of a promise from God. We saw in the previous chapter that this didn't happen through her human strength. It was a work of God's grace. Sarah had been barren her whole life, but God healed her and blessed her with a son. With this miracle came both increase and fruitfulness as well. This was all a work of God's love and grace. *"For it is written that Abraham had two sons, one by the slave woman and one by the free woman. But the son by the slave woman was born according to the flesh and the son by the free woman through the promise"* (Gal 4:22-23 NASB). When we are living out of our identity in Christ, we have access to the same blessing of increase and fruitfulness. This is our birthright as children of Sarah, who is the free woman. Sarah is a picture of the New Covenant, through which we have received the blessing of supernatural fruitfulness and increase. This is our inheritance as children of God.

Expecting Increase and Blessing

Since we are children of the free woman and have been born by the power of a promise, we should expect increase and blessing to flow from our lives all the time. This is what Sarah's change of name meant. Her identity had been so connected to barrenness and infertility before, but in changing her name, God called her to break forth and shout joyfully. She was going to be blessed with many children. She had become a princess of God!

In contrast, there is a heavenly Jerusalem above us, which is our true "mother." She is the freewoman, birthing children into freedom! For it is written: "Burst forth with gladness, rejoice, o barren woman with no children, break through with the shouts of joy and jubilee, for you are about to give birth! The one who was once considered desolate and barren now has more children than the one who has a husband!" Dear friends, just like Isaac, we're now the true children who inherit the kingdom promises (Gal. 4:26-28 TPT).

Sarah became the mother of all who are born of the promise and that refers to all of God's children. As her name was changed and she received her heavenly identity, she was being delivered from her old fallen identity of barrenness. Sarah began to embrace her new identity as the mother of a nation and a whole new people. There is power in embracing our identity in Christ.

Fruitfulness by Grace, Through Faith

As we saw in an earlier chapter, the author of Hebrews mentions Sarah in his list of heroes of faith. There we'll find the key to walk in the blessing of fruitfulness and increase all the time. *"By faith even Sarah herself received ability to conceive, even beyond the proper time of life, since she considered Him faithful who had promised"* (Hebr. 11:11 NASB). The key to bear much fruit is to live by faith. Faith empowers us to give birth to the promises of God into this world. The Father's promises are always given by grace and we receive them through faith. Living by faith is the gateway to walk in the blessing of effortless increase and fruitfulness.

This was an important key for me when I started to take steps in building the vision that God had given to me. For some reason, I lived with the impression that the way to success and increase in my calling and purpose, was to work as hard as possible. I had developed a very performance-based approach toward ministry and the building of a vision. Over time I realized that the key to breakthrough was something different. Self-effort might work in the world, but the Kingdom of God operates by different laws.

The key to live a fruitful and blessed life in the Kingdom of God is to live by grace, through faith. I have now learned how to live by grace and to walk in the blessings of fruitfulness and increase, through faith.

The Difference Between the New and the Old

One of the major differences between life in the New Covenant, compared to the old covenant, has to do with how we bear fruit. In the old covenant, fruit came by works of the law. In the New Covenant, we bear lasting fruit by grace through faith. We have seen how Sarah is a picture of the New Covenant and that she is called the free woman. Hagar is an allegorical picture of the old covenant, the slave woman.

But the son by the slave woman was born according to the flesh and the son by the free woman through the promise. This is speaking allegorically, for these women are two covenants: one coming from Mount Sinai giving birth to children who are to be slaves; she is Hagar (Gal. 4:23-24 NASB).

Hagar is called the slave woman and she gives birth by the power of the flesh. The only way to produce fruit while still living under the law is through our human strength. That will always cause us to end up in spiritual slavery. That which is born according to the flesh, needs to be fueled and maintained by the flesh. *"That which is born of the flesh is flesh and that which is born of the Spirit is spirit"* (John 3:6 NKJV). We need to remember this in our life with the Father, especially if we want to live out the vision that He has given to us.

Jesus Promises That We Will Bear Lasting Fruit

We did not choose Jesus first, but He chose us. We responded to His calling and came to Him. When Jesus called us, He promised that those of us who responded would bear an abundance of fruit that remains. *"You did not choose Me but I chose you and appointed you that you would go and bear fruit and that your fruit would remain, so that whatever you ask of the Father in My name He may give to you"* *(John 15:16 NASB).* Just like Sarah, we bear fruit by the power of God's promises. Fruitfulness is our birthright and inheritance. We receive the blessing of fruitfulness by faith in His promises.

Working from Fruitfulness

The difference between a legalistic approach to working for God, compared to working for God from a New Covenant perspective is not found in how hard we're working. Being a builder and a visionary in the Kingdom of God will involve a lot of hard work. The difference is that in the New Covenant, we work from our identity in Christ. We are already blessed with fruit that remains. In other words, we are not working to produce fruit, but resting in the fact that fruit is a blessing from the Father. This means that we can trust Him to bless the vision that He has given to us. Our job is to stay faithful to His instructions, knowing that the results of our work are His responsibility. Peace will fill our hearts when we realize that we are not responsible for the results. Instead, we bear fruit because we are in Christ.

Working Hard Under Grace

I would be lying if I told you that I never work hard. I'm involved in a lot of things and I have devoted my life fully to the cause of bringing the love of the Father and the finished work of Christ to every stream in the body of Christ. At times, this involves a lot of hard work with an intense schedule. The big difference for me is that I work hard without feeling the pressure to perform, or to please people. I'm doing what I am called to do, simply because that is what I see my Father doing. This is what it means to work under grace. Paul illustrates what it means to work hard under grace with the following statement: *"But by the [remarkable] grace of God I am what I am and His grace toward me was not without effect. In fact, I worked harder than all of the apostles, though it was not I, but the grace of God [His unmerited favor and blessing which was] with me"* (1 Cor. 15:10 AMP). There will be seasons involving a lot of hard work, but at the same time the grace of God works for us. We live in His unmerited favor and blessing, which guarantees our increase and fruitfulness.

Activations

- We started this chapter by reading Gal. 4:21-25. Spend some time reading this passage together with Jesus. Start by reading the whole passage, all at once. Read it again, this time slowly, while asking Jesus for more insight and write down what He shows you. Repeat this activation a couple of times.

- In this chapter we have seen that fruitfulness and restful increase is our birthright. Do you have a vision of what a fruitful life might look like for you? Take some time to dream about fruitfulness and increase in your calling. Invite the Holy Spirit to help you. Write a vision of how your life will look like when you bear lasting fruit.

- One of the key verses when it comes to understand how to live in the blessing of increase and fruitfulness is John 15:16. Read and pray over this verse. Ask the Holy Spirit to give revelation on this verse. Write down any insight you receive.

- Take 20-30 minutes in prayer. Ask Jesus to make you and your family fruitful. Ask Him to bless every area of your life with increase and fruitfulness.

CHAPTER 16: SPIRITUAL ISHMAELS

Before Sarah's name was changed, it's obvious that her belief was that God had caused her to be barren. Barrenness had become her identity. She was so desperate to have an heir that she came up with a plan of her own to solve this painful problem that had tormented her so much. Sarah wanted Abraham to impregnate Hagar, her slave woman.

Now Sarai, Abram's wife, had not borne him a child, but she had an Egyptian slave woman whose name was Hagar. So Sarai said to Abram, "See now, the Lord has prevented me from bearing children. Please have relations with my slave woman; perhaps I will obtain children through her." And Abram listened to the voice of Sarai (Gen. 16:1-2 NASB).

This was obviously not the Father's plan for how Isaac was to be born and neither was it His will for Sarah to be barren. This was her way of trying to accomplish the will of God in the flesh. She succumbed to this behavior because she operated out of a shame-based identity. During this time in history, it was very shameful not to be able to have a child. So, Sarah acted out of shame and desperation. But trying to fulfill the will of God through fleshly means never works out well. The result of Sarah's plan turned out to be devastating. Abraham and Hagar had a child, a boy that was named Ishmael. This caused a lot of heartache for Abraham and Sarah and it still creates problems for us even to this day.

The Orphan Heart and "Spiritual Ishmaels"

When we operate out of a fallen identity, we will always end up under the law by being conditioned to labor in our own strength to accomplish the will of God. This leads to spiritual slavery and exhaustion from managing a vision built by fleshly means. *"Now this Hagar is Mount Sinai in Arabia and corresponds to the present*

Jerusalem, for she is enslaved with her children" (Gal. 4:25 NASB). A fallen identity is the fruit of not knowing our Father. Therefore, it is always rooted in an orphan heart. Orphans are conditioned to build their platform and ministry in their own strength. Since the orphan has not been established in true sonship, they are left to fight for themselves. If we operate out of an orphan identity, we will always end up producing "spiritual Ishmaels". Here is a good definition of a spiritual Ishmael: *A spiritual Ishmael is the fruit of the believer's attempt to accomplish the will of God by their own strength.*

A spiritual Ishmael could be a ministry or a work that has been born of the flesh. As a result, it will not be blessed by the Father and must therefore be maintained through our own strength. A spiritual Ishmael may look nice and God will even bless them to a degree, but it will not be God's best for us. A spiritual Ishmael could be the fruit of our attempts to fulfill God's promises in our own way as well. *"That which is born of the flesh is flesh; and that which is born of the Spirit is spirit"* (John 3:6). Whatever is born of the flesh will need fleshly support to survive. If we try to build a spiritual work with human strength, there will be no grace for fruitfulness. We will then have to maintain the vision by our own strength and that will rob us of God's peace fast. The only way to avoid this trap is to be established in the New Covenant, while operating out of our new identity in Christ.

The Flesh Persecutes That Which Is Born of the Spirit

That which is born of the flesh can never exist in harmony with that which is born of the spirit. *"But as at that time the son who was born according to the flesh persecuted the one who was born according to the Spirit, so it is even now"* (Gal. 4:29 NASB). Paul uses the story of Ishmael and Isaac to reveal that everything that has been born of the flesh will always persecute that which is born of the spirit. That is exactly what happened between Sarah and Hagar. When Hagar had become pregnant with Ishmael, she started to treat

Sarah with contempt. *"So Abram had sexual relations with Hagar and she became pregnant. But when Hagar knew she was pregnant, she began to treat her mistress, Sarai, with contempt"* (Gen. 16:4 NLT). This led to tension and arguments between Abraham and Sarah. She started to treat Hagar so harshly that she ran away. The angel of the Lord appeared to Hagar in the wilderness and told her to return to Sarah and submit to her, which she eventually did. God gave a promise to Hagar that Ishmael would also become a great people and that he would be surrounded by conflicts with all his brothers (Gen. 16:5-12). This was a tough situation for Hagar, but in the midst of this mess, she had an encounter with the Lord that gave her a lot of comfort. She realized that God saw her and was there to watch over her and protect her (Gen. 16:13-14). This gave Hagar strength to return to Abraham and Sarah again. There she gave birth to Ishmael.

We know that Abraham and Sarah finally gave birth to their own son Isaac, the promised son and heir. When Isaac was still a child, Ishmael had already grown and become a teenager. Ishmael had lived his whole life, knowing that he wasn't the chosen son that God had promised. Of course, this was very painful for Ishmael, who carried a wound of rejection and abandonment because of this. When Isaac was about to be weaned, Abraham made a huge feast for his son and the pain of rejection within Ishmael's heart manifested as mockery and contempt for Isaac. Sarah caught him as he made fun of Isaac. He treated Isaac with the same contempt as his mother, Hagar, had earlier treated Sarah. *"When Isaac grew up and was about to be weaned, Abraham prepared a huge feast to celebrate the occasion. But Sarah saw Ishmael—the son of Abraham and her Egyptian servant Hagar—making fun of her son, Isaac"* (Gen. 21:8-9 NLT). This is a picture of how the religious system will always end up persecuting that which is born of the spirit. This usually manifests in the form of mockery, contempt, or the overbearing religious concern for balance.

Anyone who has received a genuine calling from God to birth a new vision, or to pioneer a new work in the Kingdom of God will be persecuted by the religious establishment. The churches and ministries that are built through the flesh, will almost always end up persecuting the ministries and visions that are born of the Spirit. Most of the persecution and pain that we must endure will come from religious people, who are operating out of the flesh. I have at times faced persecution, involving both physical violence and death threats, but the most painful persecution I have faced has always come from brothers and sisters in Christ who walked in the flesh. Those of us who have been called by Christ to birth something new in the Kingdom of God, need to be prepared for this as well. This principle will always remain: *That which is born of the flesh will always persecute that which is born of the Spirit.*

Throw Out the Bond Woman… and Her Son

Sarah reacted strongly when she saw how Ishmael was mocking and ridiculing Isaac. *"Now Sarah saw the son of Hagar the Egyptian, whom she had borne to Abraham, mocking Isaac. Therefore she said to Abraham, 'Drive out this slave woman and her son, for the son of this slave woman shall not be an heir with my son Isaac' (Gen. 21:9-10 NASB).* This was a hard decision to make for Abraham. He loved Ishmael, but the Lord told him to listen to Sarah (Gen. 21:11-13). Even though Hagar and Ishmael were sent away, the Lord gave some amazing promises to Abraham concerning Ishmael as well. We will come back to these promises later in this chapter, but for now, the important point to remember is that Hagar and her son were being sent away.

So Abraham got up early in the morning and took bread and a skin of water and gave them to Hagar, putting them on her shoulder and gave her the boy and sent her away. And she departed and wandered about in the wilderness of Beersheba (Gen. 21:14 NASB).

Hagar is a picture of the old covenant and Ishmael is a picture of the fruit that is born through works of the law. There is only one proper way to react, if we realize that we have allowed any part of the old covenant and its fruit to be present in our life with God. We need to drive it out from our lives. *"But what does the Scripture say? 'Drive out the slave woman and her son, for the son of the slave woman shall not be an heir with the son of the free woman.' So then, brothers and sisters, we are not children of a slave woman, but of the free woman"* (Gal. 4:30-31 NASB). Jesus is our redeemer, but He will not redeem that which is born of the flesh. The only proper response is to drive it out. We need to drive out the bond woman and her son from our lives.

What Is a Spiritual Ishmael?

A spiritual Ishmael is a ministry, activity, or some other type of work in the Kingdom of God, which is born of the flesh. It is the fruit of legalistic striving in our lives. If we want to live and work from a place of rest where we bear the kind of fruit that remains, we must drive out all legalism and its expressions from our lives. We can create a spiritual Ishmael, by allowing that which is born of the flesh in our lives and ministry, in many ways:

- ***Keeping a work or ministry going for too long.***
  Some ministries and expressions of our life with Christ, are meant to last only for a season. One way through which we can allow that which is born of the flesh in our ministries is to keep doing these activities, even if their season is over and it is time to leave them behind to birth new things.

- ***Starting something that is not born of God at all.***
  We need to be led by the Holy Spirit when we want to build something in the Kingdom of God. Starting a new ministry or activity just because it seems like a good idea, will cause us to end up with a spiritual Ishmael even if it

looks good. That which is born of the flesh remains flesh, even if it is the kind of flesh that looks good. These "good ideas" will usually end up stealing our energy and lead to exhaustion.

- ***Acting out of God's timing.***
  Another way to give birth to a spiritual Ishmael is to act outside of God's timing. Isaac and Jesus were both born at God's appointed time (Gen. 21:2, Gal. 4:4). In contrast, Ishmael was born as the result of Abraham and Sarah's attempts to fulfill God's promises in their own strength, while at the same time acting out of God's timing. This reveals to us that we can receive genuine promises from God, but if we act out of His timing, we will still end up with the fruit of the flesh.

These are all examples of ministries born through the flesh. They have one thing in common: *They will steal our time, energy and joy.* The ministries that are born of the flesh may look impressive and they might even appear fruitful, but they lack spiritual life. There will be no grace to keep that type of work going. If we have built a ministry or a vision in the flesh, we need to repent, let it die and bury it. We need to drive out all spiritual Ishmaels from our lives and ministries. We need a lot of wisdom and discernment from Jesus to know the difference between that which is born of the spirit and that which is born of the flesh.

The Blessing of Humility

It takes a lot of humility to recognize that we have tried to keep ministries going that are born according to the flesh. But once we give up on our spiritual Ishmaels and drive them out of our lives, God will honor our humility by releasing much greater measures of grace and favor upon our lives and ministries. *"But He gives a greater grace. Therefore it says, 'God is opposed to the proud, but gives grace to the humble'… Humble yourselves in the presence of the Lord and He will exalt you" (Jam. 4:6, 10 NASB).* Even if it hurts to realize that we have tried to keep something going in our own strength, this realization will teach us a lesson on humility. I have learned this lesson many times through firsthand experiences. On several occasions, I needed to realize that some of the ideas that I thought were from God, had more to do with wishful thinking. At other times, my ideas really came from God, but my way of fulfilling God's plans was not His. This has taught me the blessing of repentance and humility. The good news is that I still won in the end. I got a lesson on humility, which became a gateway for more favor to be released in my life. Since walking in humility is the pathway to the grace and favor of God, we will still end up with even more blessing and breakthrough than ever before. Our God is a good and generous Father!

Activations

- Because Sarah convinced Abraham to try to fulfill God's promises in their own strength, Ishmael was born. Have you ever had similar situations in your own life, where you tried to fulfill God's will in your own strength and had a "spiritual Ishmael"? What lessons could you learn from these mistakes? Take some time to process this and invite the Holy Spirit to speak to you on this topic. Write down the insights you receive.

- There are two scriptures mentioned within this chapter, that give important insights into why the flesh always persecutes that which is born of the Spirit:

  1. *"But as at that time the son who was born according to the flesh persecuted the one who was born according to the Spirit, so it is even now" (Gal. 4:29 NASB).*

  2. *"That which is born of the flesh is flesh; and that which is born of the Spirit is spirit" (John 3:6).*

  Take some time to meditate and pray over these verses. Ask the Father to give a deeper insight into these truths, so that you can discern the difference between the work of the Spirit and the works of the flesh. Write down the revelations you receive.

- Take 20-30 minutes in prayer. If you have discerned that you have birthed "spiritual Ishmaels", repent and hand them over to God. Ask the Holy Spirit to reveal how you have trusted in the flesh and ask Him to deliver you from all fleshly strategies.

- Take time to pray and intercede for the body of Christ. Ask Jesus to cleanse His body from fleshly strategies and all our spiritual Ishmaels. Ask Him to provide wisdom and grace for us to build ministries that are born of the Spirit.

CHAPTER 17: THE REDEMPTION OF OUR SPIRITUAL ISHMAELS

I wrote the previous chapters, by looking through the allegorical lense that Paul used in Galatians 4, where Hagar is the picture of the old covenant and Ishmael is a picture of that which is born of the flesh. He represents our futile attempts of trying to fulfill the will of God in the flesh. This gives us a very important insight to how all Kingdom work is born of the Spirit. Everything that God is doing in the New Covenant is a work of grace, birthed through the power of the Holy Spirit. Everything that is born of the flesh becomes a spiritual Ishmael. The good news is that the Father has taken our stupidity factor into the equation when it comes to His plans for our lives. He has a plan ready to redeem all our spiritual Ishmaels. This will be the topic of this chapter.

Hagar's and Ishmael's Perspective

Of course, when looking at this story from Hagar's perspective, we can probably all agree that she was treated in a horrible way. Hagar was Sarah's slave woman, who had no rights or freedom at all. Sarah decided to give Hagar as a gift to Abraham, for the sole purpose of giving him a son and heir. Hagar had no power to refuse this plan and she was basically forced into sleeping with Abraham, giving him a son that would be his and Sarah's heir. It is easy to understand why Hagar felt so much contempt and even anger towards Sarah. The tension between Hagar and Sarah became so strong that Hagar decided that she needed to escape, because of the mistreatment she endured from her mistress (Gen. 16:7). The angel of the Lord had to go and look for her. *"And he said, 'Hagar, slave of Sarai, where have you come from and where are you going?' 'I'm running away from my mistress Sarai,' she answered. Then the angel of the Lord told her, 'Go back to your mistress and submit to her'"* (Gen 16:8-9 NIV). She obeyed and returned to the harsh reality of being a servant in Abraham's household. When Ishmael was being raised, he learned that he would never be the heir, but that his birth was the shameful result of Sarah's mistake. He also learned that Isaac, his younger half-brother, was the son that God had promised to Abraham. Isaac would be Abraham's heir. Ishmael was basically raised to be an orphan who never was his father's first choice. When we look at this story from Hagar's and Ishmael's perspective, it is very easy to understand why they harbored so much bitterness and contempt for Sarah and Isaac. They had to endure an extremely unfair and painful treatment.

A Heartbreaking Moment and Divine Rescue

One of the most heartbreaking passages that can be found in the Bible is about Hagar's pain and despair. When she and Ishmael had been sent away from Abraham, they ended up wandering in the wilderness of Beersheba. When their water finally ran out, their situation seemed so hopeless that Hagar thought they were going to die. Can you feel the pain and despair in Hagar's words?

When the water in the skin was gone, she put the boy under one of the bushes. Then she went off and sat down about a bowshot away, for she thought, "I cannot watch the boy die." And as she sat there, she began to sob (Gen. 21:15-16 NIV).

Being a parent myself, I can't imagine the pain and hopelessness that I would have felt if I would be forced to watch my children go through something that terrible. But even though Ishmael had been rejected by his father, God had never forgotten about Him. Our Father is: *"…a father to the fatherless, a defender of widows, is God in his holy dwelling. God sets the lonely in families, he leads out the prisoners with singing"* (Ps. 68:5-6 NIV). Jesus will not leave us orphans. Our Father hears the cries of the forgotten and rejected. God heard Ishmael's cries and felt his despair. *"But God heard the boy crying and the angel of God called to Hagar from heaven, 'Hagar, what's wrong? Do not be afraid! God has heard the boy crying as he lies there. Go to him and comfort him, for I will make a great nation from his descendants'"* (Gen. 21:17-18 NLT). The Lord opened the eyes of Hagar, so that she found a new well of fresh water, where they could drink and receive new life (Gen. 21:19). They were rescued by a miracle of God's grace. It is highly possible that God created a divine wellspring with water in the desert and then revealed it to Hagar. He truly is the defender of the weak and the Father to the fatherless!

Raised to be an Orphaned and Unfavored Son

There is something very tragic with Ishmael's story. He was born with all odds stacked against him. He would never be the chosen heir and he wasn't the son God had promised. His life would be marked by strife and rejection with his brothers and sisters. God spoke these words concerning Ishmael: *"He (Ishmael) will be a wild donkey of a man; His hand will be against every man [continually fighting] And every man's hand against him; And he will dwell in defiance of all his brothers"* (Gen. 16:12 AMP). The life of the orphan is marked by strife and conflicts. The orphan is conditioned to create his own inheritance and identity. This was the reason for all the conflict and strife that surrounded Ishmael. That he lived in defiance to all his brothers means that he was rejected by them. He was not welcome in his father's house anymore.

I have met a lot of believers who have similar experiences. They might feel like they have been rejected by their spiritual parents. Others have suffered continual rejection from their churches and spiritual leaders, either because their ministry or vision have not been recognized, or because their experiences with Jesus don't fit the tradition of their church. A lot of the pioneers and visionaries in the body of Christ carries deep wounds, from being orphaned by spiritual leaders, who couldn't understand and support their calling and vision. Because this pain is hurting them so bad, they are living a life of strife and conflicts.

They need to be healed by receiving approval and love from our heavenly Father. They need a heavenly hug. It is important that we realize that God is a Father to the fatherless. He has a special care and compassion towards the ones who have been orphaned by parental figures. This applies to us on a spiritual level as well. Those of us who have been rejected by spiritual leadership, will be fathered by our heavenly Father, so that these wounds can be healed. He will restore our vision and give back what the devil has stolen. Our Father will open the eyes of the orphan who cries out to Him, so that the fatherless pioneer will find the wellspring of the Father's love. There the orphaned visionary will find new vision and be fully restored into sonship. This speaks of the heart of our Father in a powerful way. He will never leave us or give up on us. Even if God had to work with Isaac to forward His plan of redemption, He had a plan for Hagar and Ishmael as well.

One New Man in Christ

The good news is that in Christ, this kind of division no longer exists. Jesus broke down the wall of separation and healed the split between Ishmael and Isaac through the cross. All of us who are in Christ are now chosen and favored children of Abraham. We are one new man in Christ.

For He Himself is our peace, who has made both one and has broken down the middle wall of separation, having abolished in His flesh the enmity, that is, the law of commandments contained in ordinances, so as to create in Himself one new man from the two, thus making peace (Eph. 2:14-15 NKJV).

There is no longer any division between Jews and gentiles in the body of Christ. We are the Israel of God and we have been made into His Kingdom of priests and kings. *"Neither circumcision nor uncircumcision means anything; what counts is the new creation. Peace and mercy to all who follow this rule —to the Israel of God"* (Gal. 6:15-16 NIV). When we were born again, we became part of the

Father's family and we are the rightful heirs to all His promises. There are no walls of separation in the Father's family (Gal. 3:26-29). As believers, we are the seed of Abraham and we inherit the full blessing of the Kingdom. No one has a claim to the promises of God through their physical descent anymore. Jesus has broken down every wall of separation and we became heirs through the new birth. Since we are in Christ, we are children of the promise. *"For they are not all Israel who are of Israel, nor are they all children because they are the seed of Abraham; but, 'In Isaac your seed shall be called.' That is, those who are the children of the flesh, these are not the children of God; but the children of the promise are counted as the seed"* (Rom. 9:6-8 NKJV).

The Father Will Still Bless Our Ishmael

It is important to remember that even though God told Abraham to send Hagar and Ishmael away, He still promised to bless him. The Lord promised to make a great people out of Ishmael and to bless him mightily. This is what the angel of the Lord told Hagar concerning her son:

"I will greatly multiply your descendants so that they will be too many to count." The angel of the Lord said to her further, "Behold, you are pregnant and you will give birth to a son; and you shall name him Ishmael, because the Lord has heard your affliction. "But he will be a wild donkey of a man; his hand will be against everyone and everyone's hand will be against him; and he will live in defiance of all his brothers" (Gen. 16:10-12 NASB).

Later, when the Lord changed the names of Abraham and Sarah, He spoke to them about Isaac's birth. During that conversation, He also gave these promises concerning Ishmael: *"As for Ishmael, I will bless him also, just as you have asked. I will make him extremely fruitful and multiply his descendants. He will become the father of twelve princes and I will make him a great nation"* (Gen. 17:20 NLT).

The third time that God gave promises concerning Ishmael was during the tragic situation in the wilderness of Beersheba, when God heard Ishmael's cries for help. As the Father saved them, He encouraged Hagar with the following words: *"What troubles you, Hagar? Do not be afraid, for God has heard the voice of the boy from where he is [resting]. Get up, help the boy up and hold him by the hand, for I will make him a great nation"* (Gen. 21:17-18 AMP). God once again declared His plan to make Ishmael into a great nation. This is the grace of God in action!

He Makes All Things Work for Our Good… Even Our "Spiritual Ishmaels"

When we admit that we have walked in the flesh, our heavenly Father will redeem our Ishmaels and use them to accomplish His will in our lives. He is always looking for ways to shower us with His mercy and grace. As we have already seen, our Father takes our stupidity factor into His equation for our lives and He has a plan ready to redeem every one of our mistakes, including all our spiritual Ishmaels. *"So we are convinced that every detail of our lives is continually woven together for good, for we are his lovers who have been called to fulfill his designed purpose."* (Rom. 8:28 TPT). Humility can take us a long way in our journey with Jesus. If we are willing to humble ourselves and admit that we made mistakes, He will redeem our failures and bring beauty out of our ashes.

<h1 style="text-align:center">Activations</h1>

- In this chapter, we have looked at the story of Abraham and Isaac through Hagar's and Ishmael's perspective. Process this story of Abraham from their point of view. Try to grasp their pain and struggle in all of this. While you're processing, ask the Father to give more revelation on their perspective. Write down the insights you find.

- We read how Ishmael was raised to be an orphan, who knew that he wasn't the promised child. He was born to lose. Have you any experience of being an orphan? Have you ever been rejected by people you looked up to? How have these experiences shaped your life? Spend some time to process this with the Father. Ask Him to heal any wound of rejection in your heart.

- Make a list of your "spiritual Ishmaels". Ask the Father to redeem them and invite Him to reveal to you how the redeemed Ishmaels will look like. Our Father makes all things work together for our good and he loves to make beauty out of our ashes!

- Take 20-30 minutes in prayer for the body of Christ. Ask Him to redeem our "spiritual Ishmaels" and to fill them with new life. Ask Him to give us discernment to know how He wants to do that. If you receive a prophetic word or a vision for the body of Christ concerning this, write it down or record it.

- Take some time to pray over the prophetic word that you received during the previous activation. Ask Jesus what to do with it. Should you share it with friends, or publish it on social medias? Or maybe just pray over it? Follow His leading as soon as possible.

CHAPTER 18: FRIENDSHIP AND INFLUENCE WITH THE LORD

After Abraham had entered the covenant with the Lord and had received his new name, he knew that he was God's good friend. Abraham walked in a deep friendship with the Lord long before the New Covenant had even been established. He is called God's friend several times within the Scriptures. *"And the scripture was fulfilled which saith, Abraham believed God and it was imputed unto him for righteousness: and he was called the Friend of God"* (Jam. 2:23). Abraham walked in such deep intimacy with God that he lived in New Covenant realities, long before it had been put into place. The friendship that the Lord shared with Abraham affected how He dealt with Israel, centuries after Abraham was already dead. *"O our God, did you not drive out those who lived in this land when your people Israel arrived? And did you not give this land forever to the descendants of your friend Abraham?"* (2 Chron. 20:7 NLT, see also Isa. 41:8-9).

God has always wanted His people to walk in a close friendship with Him. Abraham models this reality in a beautiful way for us. It is fascinating how people like Abraham, David and Enoch had such a close relationship with the Lord that they walked in some new creation realities hundreds of years before Jesus had enacted the New Covenant through His blood. For example, Enoch lived in such a deep intimacy and friendship with the Lord that he was raptured before he died:

Now Enoch lived sixty-five years and fathered Methuselah. Then Enoch walked with God three hundred years after he fathered Methuselah and he fathered other sons and daughters. So all the days of Enoch were 365 years. Enoch walked with God; and he was not, for God took him (Gen. 5:21-24 NASB).

The Lord wanted to have Enoch in His presence all the time, so He simply brought Enoch home into the heavenlies. Enoch is our forerunner, who models for us just how significant and powerful an intimate relationship with Christ can really be. In fact, in the New Covenant we can walk in an even deeper friendship with Jesus, since we have been made one spirit with Him (1 Cor. 6:17). Jesus lives within us and we have instant access to Him all the time. We are His friends!

God Shares His Heart with Abraham

One day while Abraham was sitting at his tent door, relaxing in the heat of the day, some very unusual visitors came to see him. These visitors brought some good news to Abraham and a very serious one as well.

Now the Lord appeared to Abraham by the oaks of Mamre, while he was sitting at the tent door in the heat of the day. When he raised his eyes and looked, behold, three men were standing opposite him; and when he saw them, he ran from the tent door to meet them and bowed down to the ground (Gen. 18:1-2 NASB).

Abraham had a personal visit from the Lord. We can find several occasions in the Old Testament, where Jesus revealed Himself in in His preincarnate form. This was most likely one such occasion. Later, during one of His many confrontations with the religious leaders in Israel, Jesus explained to them that Abraham had seen His day: *"Your father Abraham rejoiced to see my day: and he saw it and was glad. Then said the Jews unto him, Thou art not yet fifty years old and hast thou seen Abraham? Jesus said unto them, Verily, verily, I say unto you, Before Abraham was, I am"* (John 8:56-58). Abraham walked in a deep revelation of Jesus. That he had seen the day of Christ, meant that he already knew Jesus personally, even if only to some degree. To see Him as He really is, will create a desire in our hearts to know Him more. Everything that has true value in our relationship with Jesus, always begins with a revelation of His heart.

This encounter with Jesus was very significant. We have already seen how God had spoken to Abraham several times about Isaac, his son and heir. It was during this visit that God told Abraham that his son was going to be born within a year. It was also during this conversation that Sarah laughed in unbelief (Gen. 18:9-15). We have studied these events earlier in this book. In this chapter, we will look at what happened right after this conversation.

The Lord Reveals His Secret to His Friend

After they had eaten, the Lord and His companions arose to go to Sodom. Abraham joined them for a while to say goodbye and send them off. This is when the Lord gives us a hint of how much He values true friendship with us. *"The Lord said, 'Shall I hide from Abraham what I am about to do, since Abraham will certainly become a great and mighty nation and in him all the nations of the earth will be blessed'" (Gen. 18:17-18 NASB)?* The Lord considered Abraham such a good friend that He couldn't hide His plans from him. But friendship with the Lord can go even deeper than just knowing His secrets. Abraham was able to influence the outcome of God's plan, by sharing his heart with the Lord in prayer.

The Lord Listens to Abraham

Before He left to visit Sodom and Gomorrah, the Lord shared His concerns for these ungodly cities with Abraham.

"And the Lord said, 'The outcry of Sodom and Gomorrah is indeed great and their sin is exceedingly grave. I will go down now and see whether they have done entirely as the outcry, which has come to Me indicates; and if not, I will know'" (Gen. 18:20-21 NASB).

When God shared His plan for Sodom and Gomorrah, Abraham immediately asked if the Lord really was going to destroy even the righteous, together with the wicked (Gen. 18:22-24). He then elaborates on why it would be a bad idea for the Lord to do so:

Far be it from You to do such a thing, to kill the righteous with the wicked, so that the righteous and the wicked are treated alike. Far be it from You! Shall not the Judge of all the earth deal justly? So the Lord said, "If I find in Sodom fifty righteous within the city, then I will spare the entire place on their account" (Gen. 18:25-26 NASB).

The Lord agreed with Abraham and promised to spare the cities if He could find these fifty righteous people within the city. There is power in our intercession to influence both the heart and plans of God. Abraham did not stop with fifty. He kept on asking the Lord to spare the cities if He could find forty-five, then forty and thirty. The Lord granted Abraham this request as well. Abraham continued by asking the Lord to spare Sodom if twenty righteous people could be found in there. Abraham kept pressing on all the way down to ten righteous people. God listened to Abraham and promised to spare the city if there were even ten righteous people to be found within the city (Gen. 18:22-33). The Lord was deeply touched by the pleading of Abraham.

Sodom and Gomorrah Were Destroyed

Sadly, God couldn't find ten righteous people within the cities of Sodom and Gomorrah. Therefore, the Lord destroyed these cities through a heavy rain of fire and brimstone (Gen. 19:23-29). These two cities have since become a symbol of the fate of the wicked, who will perish in the lake of fire and face eternal death. This was a very tragic and sobering event. I have often wondered how Abraham felt when he woke up the next morning and realized what had happened.

Now Abraham got up early in the morning and went to the place where he had stood before the Lord; and he looked down toward Sodom and Gomorrah and toward all the land of the surrounding area; and behold, he saw the smoke of the land ascended like the smoke of a furnace (Gen 19:27-28 NASB).

The sight of these ruined cities must have been a terrifying vision to behold. Abraham's thoughts must have been with his nephew. Lot had chosen the valley where these cities had been built as his part of the land.

Lot Was Rescued Because of God's Covenant with Abraham

Abraham didn't need to worry for Lot. God knew that Abraham wanted Lot to be spared. *"So it came about, when God destroyed the cities of the surrounding area, that God remembered Abraham and sent Lot out of the midst of the destruction, when He overthrew the cities in which Lot had lived" (Gen 19:29 NASB).* Because of His friendship with Abraham, the Lord saved Lot from the destruction of these cities, but Lot and his family still suffered terrible losses. Even though Lot and his daughters were rescued, he lost his wife and his daughters lost their husbands in the destruction of the cities. Another consequence of their time living in Sodom, was that all of them had been influenced by the iniquity of this ungodly city. Lot's family were damaged and broken in a very tragic way as a consequence of their time living in Sodom (Luke 19:15-38). The two daughters of Lot even had him drunk and slept with him to have kids. But the good news in all of this was that they survived.

Lot and his daughters were rescued because of Abraham's close friendship with the Lord. Being a friend of God will affect all our relationships in a deep way. There is redeeming power and grace in our relationship with God that will benefit our loved ones as well. I wonder what would have happened if Abraham had kept on stretching his request for Sodom to be spared even further? It is not unlikely that these cities could have been saved.

We Are Friends of Christ

That Jesus wants to share the secrets of His heart with us is the essence of friendship with God. Jesus expressed this reality when He said that He wants to share everything that He hears from the Father with us. *"Henceforth I call you not servants; for the servant knoweth not what his lord doeth: but I have called you friends; for all things that I have heard of my Father I have made known unto you"* *(John 15:15).* For Jesus, this is the sign of true friendship. As we're responding to the invitation into friendship with Jesus, our lives will impact the people around us in a very powerful way. Living in intimate friendship with Jesus will release the presence of God to draw people to the Father. This actually means that soaking in His presence is a form of evangelism.

Because friendship with Jesus doesn't sound that practical, we can underestimate how much a friend of Jesus can influence this world. Abraham is probably one of the best examples of this. We are friends of Jesus and our prayers influence the heart of God. This means that we can have huge impact on this world and the church through our prayers. This reveals the humility of Jesus. He is prepared to listen to us when we share our heart with Him. Through prayer and intercession, we can partner with Him in extending the Kingdom of God. Jesus have even left a part of the future open to be influenced by our choices, where we will be part of deciding the outcome of certain events. This is how much Jesus trusts His friends!

Intercession for the Body of Christ

Abraham shows us an important aspect of being the Lord's good friend, when He intercedes for the righteous men and women to be saved from the destruction of Sodom and Gomorrah. This is exactly what Jesus is doing for us right now in the heavenlies. He is praying for us. *"Who is he that condemneth? It is Christ that died, yea rather, that is risen again, who is even at the right hand of God, who also maketh intercession for us" (Rom. 8:34).* Jesus is our high priest, who is always interceding for us, praying that the Father's plans and purposes will be fulfilled in our lives. Being good friends of Jesus Christ, we are called to do the same. A lifestyle of prayer and intercession reveal a Christlike heart.

I have realized that it's never enough for just me and my family to be blessed. We need the whole body of Christ to live in all the benefits and blessings of the New Covenant. That is the only way for us to fulfill the great commission and become everything that God has called us to be. Until that has happened, we need to pray and intercede for the whole body of Christ, just like Jesus is doing right now. *"Wherefore he is able also to save them to the uttermost that come unto God by him, seeing he ever liveth to make intercession for them" (Hebr. 7:25).*

New Covenant Worldview

In the New Covenant, our Father relates differently to the world, compared to the way He did in the old covenant. This is because Jesus took away the sins of the world on the cross. The Father no longer holds the sins of the world against it. *"All this is from God, who reconciled us to himself through Christ and gave us the ministry of reconciliation: that God was reconciling the world to himself in Christ, not counting people's sins against them. And he has committed to us the message of reconciliation" (2 Cor. 5:18-19 NIV).* Our Father will not judge the world today in the same way that He did with Sodom and Gomorrah. Instead, He wants all the ungodly cities of the world to be saved and transformed by the gospel of Jesus.

Jesus even told us how this could happen. *"Woe to you, Chorazin! Woe to you, Bethsaida! For if the miracles that were performed in you had been performed in Tyre and Sidon, they would have repented long ago in sackcloth and ashes" (Matt. 11:21 NIV).* Tyre and Sidon were very ungodly cities, but Jesus reveals that if someone would have gone there to minister in the power of the Holy Spirit, these cities would have repented. As Jesus continues to speak, He mentions Capernaum and Sodom, which we are familiar with from earlier studies of this chapter. *"And you, Capernaum, will you be lifted to the heavens? No, you will go down to Hades. For if the miracles that were performed in you had been performed in Sodom, it would have remained to this day"* (Matt. 11:23 NIV). Jesus shows us that the key for these ungodly cities to be saved is the miracle-ministry, in the power of the Holy Spirit. Signs and wonders will open even the ungodly cities of the world to the gospel. We are not called to ask God to judge the ungodly people and nations of this world. The disciples already tried that in Samaria and they were rebuked by Jesus for suggesting such a thing.

"Lord, do You want us to command fire to come down from heaven and consume them, just as Elijah did? But He turned and rebuked them and said, 'You do not know what manner of spirit you are of. For the Son of Man did not come to destroy men's lives but to save them.' And they went to another village (Luke 9:54-56 NKJV).

In the New Covenant, we are called to preach the gospel of Jesus with signs and wonders, so that people can receive new life from Him and get saved. Our Father is always longing to bring all His lost children back home again. He even wants to partner with us in that endeavor. We don't have to plead with God to spare our nations and cities. There is no judgement coming from heaven in the New Covenant. The Father only has grace and salvation to give to the world. Let's preach the gospel and partner with Jesus to bring the ungodliest and darkest cities in the world back home to the Father through Jesus Christ!

<h1 style="text-align:center">Activations</h1>

- Abraham is an old covenant example of friendship with God. In the New Covenant, every believer is a friend of Jesus. How does this reality affect your identity and your relationship with Jesus? Take some time to reflect on this reality. Invite the Holy Spirit to reveal more about your friendship with Jesus. Write down any new insight that you might receive.

- We saw how the essence of friendship with Jesus is that He shares His secrets with us. Invite Jesus to share some secrets with you right now. Write down what He reveals to you. But don't share it unless He leads you to do so.

- An important part of friendship with Jesus is to carry the heart of an intercessor. Take 20-30 minutes in prayer. Ask the Father to fill your life with the Spirit of prayer. Ask Him to give you an intercessors heart and to purify your heart from all accusation and condemnation.

- In the New Covenant, our Father doesn't judge the cities like He did in the old covenant. The way that He relates to the world changed, because Jesus nailed the sins of the world to the cross and reconciled all of humanity to the Father. We can see this by studying these Scriptures:

   1. *2 Cor. 5:17-21*
   2. *John 1:29, 36*
   3. *1 John 2:1-2*

Read these Scriptures and reflect on them. Take some time to process what you find together with Jesus. Write down what He shows you.

- Take 20-30 minutes in prayer. Intercede for the big cities of the world. Jesus promised us that if the same miracles that He did, were to be done in the big, immoral cities in the world like Sodom and Gomorrah, these cities would be saved. Ask the Father to raise up many missionaries, who walk in the realm of miracles, within the big cities of the world. Ask the Father for a big harvest of souls to be brought into the Kingdom of God from the ungodliest cities in the world.

CHAPTER 19: SACRIFICING THE PROMISE

There is a very famous event in Abraham's journey with the Lord that we haven't paid much attention to so far in this book, but we will look at it right now. This event is a prophetic picture of the finished work of Christ, as well as a foreshadowing of a spiritual principle that all of us must learn, sooner or later in our life with Jesus. The book of Hebrews describes this event in the following way:

By faith Abraham, when he was tested, offered up Isaac and he who had received the promises offered up his only begotten son, of whom it was said, "In Isaac your seed shall be called," concluding that God was able to raise him up, even from the dead, from which he also received him in a figurative sense (Hebr. 11:17-19 NKJV).

The event described in this passage have caused many believers to scratch their heads, wondering what was going on. Abraham had finally received his long-awaited son and heir, but suddenly God tells Him to offer Isaac as a sacrifice on mount Moriah.

A Test of Obedience

It is not as hard to understand what God was doing here, as some people might think. In fact, the Bible explains God's intentions in a simple way. This was the Lord's way to test Abraham's heart:

Some time later, God tested Abraham's faith. "Abraham!" God called. "Yes," he replied. "Here I am." "Take your son, your only son—yes, Isaac, whom you love so much—and go to the land of Moriah. Go and sacrifice him as a burnt offering on one of the mountains, which I will show you (Gen. 22:1-2 NLT).

God wanted to know what was most important to Abraham. So, the Lord tested his heart to find out if their friendship still was the most important thing in Abraham's life. We will have to face this same test several times in our lives as well. Whenever we are responding to God's calling, His promises will sooner or later be fulfilled in our lives. We will indeed live a very blessed life. The challenge that comes with living in God's blessing is that they can become our idol. If that happens, our main concern will shift from intimacy with the Lord, into keeping the vision going. That will ruin our hearts and make it impossible to live a lifestyle of abiding in the love of the Father. To keep this from happening to us, Jesus will take us through tests that reveal what we have in our hearts.

The Faithfulness of Abraham

Abraham passed this test with flying colors. He obeyed the Lord immediately. *"So Abraham got up early in the morning and saddled his donkey and took two of his young men with him and his son Isaac; and he split wood for the burnt offering and set out and went to the place of which God had told him"* (Gen. 22:3 NASB). Early the next morning, Abraham took Isaac and started his journey to Moriah. Abraham loved his son more than anything in this world, but he loved the Lord even more, so he didn't hesitate. Again, Abraham is a good example for us. When we are being tested by the Lord, we should obey as quickly as we possibly can.

The best way to find freedom to obey God is to hold our vision with open hands. We do that by making sure that we have our identity firmly rooted in Christ. We need to be rooted in the love of the Father and realize that our value and approval come from Him alone. That will always be the main thing. When we do that, we will be free to lay down our dreams and visions if God should ever call us to do that.

Trusting God for a Resurrection

We read earlier about Abraham: *"He considered that God is able to raise people even from the dead, from which he also received him back as a type" (Hebr. 11:17 NASB)*. His faith was clearly demonstrated by how certain he was that both Isaac and he would return to the camp after they had worshiped the Lord together. *"Then Abraham said to his young men, "Stay here with the donkey and I and the boy will go over there; and we will worship and return to you" (Gen. 22:5 NASB)*. Abraham knew God's heart and that He could raise Isaac back to life if necessary. A little later in this story, Abraham once again showed his unwavering trust in the Lord. As him and Isaac were walking up to mount Moriah, Isaac had a question for his father.

Isaac spoke to his father Abraham and said, "My father!" And he said, "Here I am, my son." And he said, "Look, the fire and the wood, but where is the lamb for the burnt offering. Abraham said, "God will provide for Himself the lamb for the burnt offering, my son." So the two of them walked on together (Gen. 22:7-8 NASB).

We don't exactly know how much Isaac really knew about what the Lord had spoken to Abraham. He probably didn't even know that God had told his father to sacrifice him, but Abraham gave a very prophetic answer to Isaac's question. His answer pointed to the Lamb of God, who had been slain before the foundation of the world. The Father really did provide a lamb as a sacrifice that took away the sins of the world!

They finally reached the place that God had chosen as the place of sacrifice and they built the altar there. Abraham took his son, bound him and placed him on the altar. At the last moment, just before Abraham was to kill Isaac, the angel of the Lord stopped Abraham. *"And Abraham reached out with his hand and took the knife to slaughter his son. But the angel of the Lord called to him from heaven and said, 'Abraham, Abraham!' And he said, 'Here I am' (Gen. 22:10-*

11 NASB). Abraham was ready to obey God all the way. He was prepared to sacrifice his own son and future, just to stay faithful to God. This shows us what a man of God Abraham really was. *"He said, 'Do not reach out your hand against the boy and do not do anything to him; for now I know that you fear God, since you have not withheld your son, your only son, from Me'" (Gen 22:12 NASB).*

God Provided a Sacrifice

After the angel had stopped Abraham from sacrificing Isaac, the lamb that God had provided was revealed. *"Then Abraham raised his eyes and looked and behold, behind him was a ram caught in the thicket by its horns; and Abraham went and took the ram and offered it up as a burnt offering in the place of his son" (Gen. 22:13 NASB).* This reveals an important principle. Isaac represented God's promise and through him, Abraham's dreams and visions were going to be fulfilled. When we are so free on the inside that we can allow our visions, dreams and calling to die, our Father will fill us with resurrection power. When we live with the revelation that He is our true provider, we don't need to fight to keep our work and ministry alive. This is the main reason that Abraham got a deeper revelation of God as His provider after he had passed this test. *"And Abraham named that place The Lord Will Provide, as it is said to this day, 'On the mountain of the Lord it will be provided'" (Gen. 22:14 NASB).*

My wife and I have surrendered our work to God many times. It is good for us to remind ourselves that our visions and ministries are His. We only steward them and it is important that our work never become more important to us than Jesus Himself. This is why this story gives us such a powerful lesson on what it means to give up our own rights to follow the Lamb. It is very liberating to realize that our identity is in Christ and that He is responsible for His own work. Most of the time when we are led to lay down our vision before the cross, our work will be resurrected and we will become even more fruitful. Abraham and Isaac returned to their servants alive and well (Gen. 22:19).

A Powerful Picture of the Cross

This whole story is a prophetic picture of the cross. As we read the words that God spoke to Abraham, we can see the reference to an even greater sacrifice to come. God said: *"Take now your son, your only son, whom you love, Isaac and go to the land of Moriah and offer him there as a burnt offering on one of the mountains of which I will tell you" (Gen. 22:1 NASB).* When the Father spoke about His own firstborn Son, He uses similar words.

And as Jesus rose up out of the water, the heavenly realm opened up over him and he saw the Holy Spirit descend out of the heavens and rest upon him in the form of a dove. Then suddenly the voice of the Father shouted from the sky, saying, "This is my Son—the Beloved! My greatest delight is in him" (Matt. 3:16-17 TPT).

The big difference was that when the Father had to sacrifice His Son, His only Son, the one whom He loved, there was no other lamb to sacrifice. When Abraham told Isaac that God was going to provide a lamb as a sacrifice, he was prophesying about Jesus Christ and His sacrifice on the cross. He is the lamb of God that took away the sins of the world once and for all. Through Jesus Christ, we have received the Father's full provision and blessing.

Activations

- In this chapter, we read about how God tested Abraham by telling him to sacrifice Isaac. Spend time studying this event, by reading Gen. 22:1-19. Read it a couple of times together with the Holy Spirit. Ask Him to speak to you through this story. Write down the new insights that you receive.

- There are many examples in the Bible of how the Father tested His people. Find at least three more examples of people who were tested in a similar way as Abraham. Study their story together with Jesus. Write down what He reveals to you.

- We saw how the Lord spoke to Abraham to test his heart. Have you ever been tested by Jesus in a similar way? Did you pass or fail at these tests? What did these tests reveal about your motives and heart? Take some time to reflect on this together with the Father. Write down what you discover while reflecting.

- Take 20-30 minutes in prayer. Make this time of prayer a time of surrender to Christ. Surrender your life to Jesus and specifically your calling, dreams and visions. Invite the Father to test your heart and reveal your motives. Ask Him to purify your motives.

- Take some time to intercede for the body of Christ. Ask the Father to test us and reveal our motives. Ask Him to purify us from all idolatry and to baptize us in His love.

CHAPTER 20: BURYING THE OLD SEASON

Sooner or later, we will have to face the death of an old season in our work and ministry. Not only will we have to let go of the bad seasons of life. There also comes a time when what once worked and produced good fruit for us, dies and needs to be buried. That can be very painful. Abraham experienced this when Sarah died. *"Now Sarah lived 127 years; these were the years of the life of Sarah. Sarah died in Kiriath-arba (that is, Hebron) in the land of Canaan; and Abraham came in to mourn for Sarah and to weep for her" (Gen 23:1-2 NASB).* Abraham and Sarah had lived a long, fruitful and very blessed life together. Sure, like all of us, they had to walk through seasons of sadness, pain and struggle, but through it all they had lived with the Lord, pursuing their calling and vision, but now Sarah was dead. Abraham was mourning and weeping over the loss of his wife.

Knowing When to Bury the Old Season

It takes wisdom to know when to stand in faith for God to bless a work and vision, or when it is time to bury it. It can be painful to realize that something we have invested a lot of time building and that God has blessed in the past, now is dying and needs to be buried. It is necessary to learn this if we want to stay fresh in our life with God and live with a fresh vision. Abraham needed to hold on to this truth during the painful loss of his wife. He had to learn how to walk through this season of death. *"Then Abraham arose from mourning before his dead and spoke to the sons of Heth, saying, 'I am a stranger and a foreign resident among you; give me a burial site among you so that I may bury my dead out of my sight'"* (Gen. 22:3-4 NASB). Abraham knew that he had walked through a season of mourning, but now that season was coming to an end and he needed to move on with God. To do that, Abraham had to let go of the old seasons he had shared with Sarah. Sometimes, the only way to bear fruit that remain in the Kingdom of God is to bury the work that God used in the previous season.

Bury the Old Season with Dignity

Abraham lived as a stranger in the land, so he didn't own much land himself. Therefore, he wanted to buy a piece of land to bury his wife. The inhabitants of the land held Abraham in very high esteem. They wanted to give him the burial site for free, so that he could bury his wife. However, Abraham refused to accept that offer. He wanted to bury his wife with dignity. He found a grave site that suited him well, at the cave of Machpelah (Gen. 23:5-18). Abraham bought it for full price from Ephron, who had been the previous owner. *"After this, Abraham buried his wife Sarah in the cave of the field of Machpelah facing Mamre (that is, Hebron), in the land of Canaan. So the field and the cave that was in it were deeded over to Abraham for a burial site by the sons of Heth"* (Gen 23:19 NASB). Abraham found the grave site he wanted and buried Sarah there. When we bury our old, fruitful season with dignity, it becomes a memorial site that becomes a source of praise and gratefulness to our Father.

One example of this in my own life was when we had to bury a vision that had been very fruitful. When I moved up to the north of Sweden, we started retreats that we chose to call "weekend of healing". We did these weekends all over the north. Hundreds of people came to get healed and set free during these retreats. I had trained several prayer teams to minister at these weekends. These teams helped me to minister healing and restoration to the people. Every participant was offered a counselling session and we received many moving and powerful testimonies from these weekends. Even while I am writing about these weekends now, I'm tearing up a little. After a couple of very good years of doing these weekends of healing, the Holy Spirit revealed to us that the season of ministering healing in this way was coming to an end.

We knew that the message of inner healing and restoration is an eternal part of the gospel, but our expressions of ministry are not. We realized that we had to bury this season. Because we buried it with dignity, it has now become a memorial site for us that has become a source of both gratefulness and thanksgiving to God. We still do most of our ministry in the areas of inner healing and personal restoration, but the way we do it today is different. We are more fruitful and effective in the way we minister today, but I will always look back at this season with a lot of gratitude and joy. It was a wonderful time.

Discerning When the Season of Death Is Here

Solomon expresses this truth in the book of Ecclesiastes: *"There is an appointed time for everything. And there is a time for every matter under heaven— A time to give birth and a time to die; A time to plant and a time to uproot what is planted. A time to kill and a time to heal; A time to tear down and a time to build up"* (Ecc. 3:1-3 NASB). There are different seasons in our lives and ministries. While much is being said about birthing a new vision, or taking new steps with God, it is equally important to know when it is time to let things die. Sometimes we need to tear down old expressions of ministry so that something new can be built.

I have observed that people are sometimes looking for formulas that show them what season they are presently in, but there are no such formulas. To discern our present or coming seasons, we need to be led by the Holy Spirit. This is the only way to know the Father's timing. The good news is that the Holy Spirit is more than willing to help us with this. He is an expert at helping us to live in God's timing.

The Futility and Bondage of Keeping a Dead Work Going

Dead traditions are formed when a ministry or church refuses to let go of an expression of ministry that once worked, but now has lost all life. This leads to religious bondages and the people who get stuck in trying to keep a dead ministry going will feel drained of spiritual life. Some of the best decisions Linda and I have made with Jesus was to stop doing things that no longer bore fruit for us. It is very liberating to bury old things and enter a new season with God. Quickly after burying the old seasons, new creativity and life usually birthed in our life and ministry. Unfortunately, we have also seen how some believers, churches and ministries have lost both life and creativity because they stubbornly refused to give up something that they should have buried a long time ago. A lot of the legalism and religion prevalent in the body of Christ is born in this way.

New Wine in Old Wineskins

This will result in the type of mess that Jesus spoke about within the following parable: *"Neither do people pour new wine into old wineskins. If they do, the skins will burst; the wine will run out and the wineskins will be ruined. No, they pour new wine into new wineskins and both are preserved"* (Matt. 9:17 NIV). New life always needs to be poured into our new season. If we receive new revelation and try to make it fit within our old season, it will ruin everything in the same way that new wine in old wineskins causes it to burst. We need to pour new life into every new season of our lives with the Father. It is important to realize that our expressions of doing ministry are always negotiable, but having revelation or new life is not. We need the life of Christ to thrive and live in renewal.

Being Pruned for More Fruitfulness

To bury the old season, so that we can live in the new season that God is bringing us into is the only way for us to keep bearing good fruit throughout our lives. This is what Jesus is addressing with this statement: *"I am the true grapevine and my Father is the gardener. He cuts off every branch of mine that doesn't produce fruit and he prunes the branches that do bear fruit so they will produce even more" (John 15:1-2).* Being pruned can at times feel painful and even be a little humiliating, but it's never meant as a punishment. The Father is our personal gardener, who prunes us so that we can bear more fruit. If we hadn't stopped doing the weekends of healing that I mentioned earlier, we would probably have missed many of the breakthroughs that we're seeing today.

A Personal Season of Pruning

One season of pruning that challenged me personally quite a lot, happened during the lockdown that was connected to the Covid-19 pandemic in 2020. At that time, I was busy traveling all over Scandinavia and in many other parts of the world to preach the gospel. It was a great season for me and I really enjoyed traveling and blessing churches. But then the coronavirus started to spread and the lockdown began. Within a week after all this started, almost all my trips were cancelled. As we were asking God what to do next, He led me to start writing books and minister online.

I had almost no experience at all with online ministry and even less experience of writing and publishing books, so this season humbled me in many ways. I was stretched quite a lot. The truth is that I needed to go through that season of pruning. This season brought much good and lasting fruit. My books and our online schools are now a very crucial part of our ministry. We receive a steady flow of testimonies from people who share how their lives have been transformed by our podcasts, books and our online ministry. Pruning always leads to more lasting fruit. This is the main reason that we need to bury our old seasons. Our Father is our personal gardener, who brings us into new seasons of favor and fruitfulness!

Activations

- In this chapter, we have studied the need to bury our old seasons, so that we can enter the new seasons that Christ has prepared for us. Have you ever been challenged to leave an old season behind? Was that a fruitful or a dry season? Does Jesus challenge you to do that right now? Take some time to reflect on this with Jesus. Write down what He reveals to you.

- We read Matt. 9:17 earlier in this chapter. In that passage, Jesus addressed the need for us to leave the old season to enter the new thing that God is doing. Let's read this passage from another translation:

  And who would mend worn-out clothing with new fabric? When the new cloth shrinks it will rip, making the hole worse than before. And who would pour fresh, new wine into an old wineskin? Eventually the wine will ferment and make the wineskin burst, losing everything—the wine is spilled and the wineskin ruined. Instead, new wine is always poured into a new wineskin so that both are preserved (Matt. 9:16-17 TPT).

  Take some time to pray and meditate upon these verses. Invite the Holy Spirit to give you new insight into these truths and ask the Father to prepare your heart, so that you can bury the old season when He calls you to move on with Jesus.

- We have seen how we will walk through many different seasons in our life with Christ. We read from Ecclesiastes 3:1-8 about these seasons. Take time to study and reflect upon this passage and invite the Holy Spirit to speak to you. Study the topic of times and seasons in the Bible.

- Take 20-30 minutes in prayer. Surrender your times and seasons to Jesus. If you know that you have been holding on to old expressions or activities too long, hand them over to the Father. Tell Him that that you now are ready to leave the old season to enter the new one.

CHAPTER 21: EMBRACING THE NEW SEASON

We have now come to the last chapter of Abraham's journey. He had now become an old man, who had lived a long, blessed and very fruitful life. The Bible summarizes his life with these words: *"Now Abraham was old, advanced in age; and the Lord had blessed Abraham in every way" (Gen. 24:1 NASB).* Abraham had matured into becoming the father of faith that God had foretold he would one day become. His focus was now mainly on the future of his son Isaac. Abraham wanted to find a bride for his son. He wanted to pass on as many generational blessings as possible to Isaac and he wanted his son to be fruitful and multiply.

As we keep building the vision that God has given to us, we will become increasingly more focused on sharing the blessings that we have received with other people. This is a sign of our spiritual growth. When we start walking in our calling, we usually begin by breaking new ground in the spirit and by taking new territory for God. But after we have become rooted and grounded in our calling, our focus will shift into training the next generation and to pass on our generational blessings to them.

Finding the Right Bride

As previously mentioned, the first concern that Abraham had for Isaac was to find the right bride for him. So, to get this done right, he sent his most trusted servant on this mission. *"He said to the senior servant in his household, the one in charge of all that he had" (Gen. 24:2 NIV).* It is common belief that this servant was Eliezer, the man whom Abraham had elected as his heir, before Isaac was born (Gen. 15:2). Finding a bride for Isaac was now at the top of Abraham's priorities. This shows us how much Abraham trusted this servant, but he sent him on this important mission with some very specific instructions. The bride of Isaac couldn't under any circumstances be a Canaanite woman. She had to come from the land of Ur, Abraham's own country and family. The servant was sent back there to find a wife for Isaac (Gen. 24:4). If this woman who was chosen to be the bride of Isaac, proved to be unwilling to follow the servant back to the land of Canaan, he was set free from his oath (Gen. 24:5-9). With these instructions in mind, the servant travelled all the way to Abraham's home country to find a suitable bride for Isaac.

The Servant Prays for a Successful Mission

As the servant arrived at Mesopotamia, he stopped at the well of the city to feed and to give water to his animals. There he prayed and asked God for the grace to be successful in his task. *"And he said, 'Lord, God of my master Abraham, please grant me success today and show kindness to my master Abraham'" (Gen. 24:12 NASB).* To pray and trust in God is the way forward in the Kingdom of God, whether we're building a vision or any other type of ministry for Jesus. The prayer of faith leads to breakthrough and favor (Mark. 11:23-24). The servant asked God for a specific sign in his search. He was to ask the young women that came from the city to give him some of their water to drink. The woman who offered to give water both to him and his camels, was God's chosen bride for Isaac (Gen. 24:13-14). While he was praying this simple prayer, the Lord was already sending the answer.

The Chosen Woman Is Revealed

Even before the servant had finished his simple prayer, a young and very beautiful woman came to give water to her camels. Her name was Rebekah and she did exactly the thing that the servant had asked for as a sign. She gave him water to drink and watered his camels as well. Rebekah revealed to the servant that she was the granddaughter of Abraham's brother, Nahor (Gen. 24:15-26). The servant gave many generous gifts to Rebekah and he bowed down in worship to God. *"And he said, 'Blessed be the Lord, the God of my master Abraham, who has not abandoned His kindness and His trustworthiness toward my master; as for me, the Lord has guided me in the way to the house of my master's brothers'"* (Gen. 24:27 NASB). Rebekah ran all the way back to her home to tell her family what had happened at the well. Her brother Laban ran back to the well and greeted the servant. Laban invited him to follow him to the home of Nahor. There they were to have dinner together and the servant was going to stay there as their guest (Gen.24:28-32).

Rebekah Is Brought Back to the Promised Land

Laban and the rest of his family received the servant with joy and gave him a warm welcome. Before they had dinner together, he shared with them what had happened. They realized that this was the Lord's plan, so they all agreed that Rebekah could travel with the servant back to Canaan and marry Isaac (Gen. 24:33-58). But before she left, her family blessed her in a powerful way:

Our sister, may you increase to thousands upon thousands; may your offspring possess the cities of their enemies (Gen 24:59 NIV).

As we have seen throughout this book, it is powerful to declare blessings and speak the promises of God over a person. Decrees and blessings release the will of the Lord and His creative power to work for us. I suggest that you make it a habit to declare what God has spoken over your own life, as well as over your family and ministry. This is a powerful way to partner with the Lord in releasing His will for your life!

Isaac Marries Rebekah

The servant brought Rebekah to the home of Abraham in Negev and as they came closer, they saw Isaac from a distance. He was out strolling and meditating in the fields. She covered her face, as not to let her face be seen by him and greeted him (Gen. 24:62-66). The servant told him about what had happened throughout his journey. *"Then Isaac brought her into his mother Sarah's tent and he took Rebekah and she became his wife and he loved her; so Isaac was comforted after his mother's death" (Gen. 24:67 NASB).* And the rest is history!

A Prophetic Picture of Christ and His Bride

The story of Isaac and Rebekah is one of the clearest pictures of Jesus and His bride that we can find within the Scriptures. In this story, Isaac is a type of Jesus. He is the seed of Abraham, the son of promise. In Galatians, Paul shows us that Jesus Himself is the only true seed of Abraham: *"Now to Abraham and his seed were the promises made. He saith not and to seeds, as of many; but as of one and to thy seed, which is Christ" (Gal. 3:16).* Abraham is a type of the Father, since He desires for His son to have a bride and sends a servant to find her in a foreign country. That servant is a type of the Holy Spirit who is sent by the Father into the world to find and prepare a beautiful bride for the Son. Of course, Rebekah is a picture of us, the bride of Christ. The union between Isaac and Rebekah became very fruitful. Their offspring brought salvation into this world, through the birth of Christ. Our union with Jesus is fruitful as well. Through our union with Jesus, salvation goes forth everywhere. The whole world will be blessed through us!

Abraham Remarries but Sends Away the Other Sons

In his later years, Abraham married Keturah and they had both sons and grandchildren together (Gen. 25:1-4). Some people have claimed that Keturah and Hagar are the same woman, but I have never found any biblical proof backing up this claim. What we do know for sure is that the sons Abraham had with Keturah had to leave, just like Ishmael. They were sent away to the land of the east. Then Abraham gave everything he had to Isaac, the son of promise. *"Now Abraham gave all that he had to Isaac; but to the sons of his concubines, Abraham gave gifts while he was still living and sent them away from his son Isaac eastward, to the land of the east" (Gen.*

25:5-6 NASB). We can see how important it became for Abraham that Isaac inherited everything he had. He made sure that Isaac would walk in a level of blessing and fruitfulness that surpassed what Abraham himself had ever experienced.

Blessed and Satisfied with Life

As we saw in the beginning of this chapter, Abraham had been blessed with a long, exciting and very fruitful life. *"These are all the years of Abraham's life that he lived, 175 years. Abraham breathed his last and died at a good old age, an old man and satisfied with life; and he was gathered to his people" (Gen. 25:7-8 NASB).* When the Bible says that Abraham died as an old man and satisfied with life, it reveals that he finished well. It is rather easy to start well, but to keep on walking with God for the rest of our lives is way more challenging. Abraham did that. He made a couple of painful and costly mistakes and he had to walk through some rough seasons with the Lord, but he remained faithful through it all. This is the reason that he is called the father of our faith today.

Abraham Is Buried with Sarah

Isaac and Ishmael buried Abraham in the grave their father had bought for his wife Sarah. *"Then his sons Isaac and Ishmael buried him in the cave of Machpelah, in the field of Ephron the son of Zohar the Hittite, facing Mamre, the field which Abraham purchased from the sons of Heth; there Abraham was buried with his wife Sarah (Gen. 25:9-10 NASB).* Abraham and Sarah shared a long life together. Now they were reunited in death as well.

Isaac and Ishmael came together to bury their father. This was an exciting reunion. Isaac was God's chosen heir, but the Lord had promised to bless Ishmael as well. He also became the father of a people and he was a blessed man. That Isaac and Ishmael could bury Abraham together is a prophetic sign, pointing to how our Father has removed all enmity through Jesus and made us into one new man (Eph. 2:14-18). Through the offspring of Abraham, the Lord had promised that all the nations were to be blessed. His faith in God impacted the whole world! Today we can see the consequences of the blessing of Abraham in a much greater way. The Kingdom of God keeps growing in a powerful way. We are now living in very exciting times.

Isaac Was Blessed by God

Even after Abraham was dead and buried, his life and devotion to God still impacted the world through Isaac, his son and chosen heir. *"It came about after the death of Abraham, that God blessed his son Isaac; and Isaac lived by Beer-lahai-roi" (Gen. 25:11 NASB).* Isaac grew up to become a blessed and powerful man, who walked in the fullness of the generational blessings, which he had inherited from Abraham. These same blessings are given to us who are in Jesus Christ (Gal. 3:13-14).

Turn the Hearts of the Fathers Back to the Children

Abraham had a father's heart toward his son. It is one thing to be someone's physical father, but it is something else to grow up to have a father's heart toward one's children. Throughout history, this has proven to be a very big challenge for the church. Most of the time, the older generation of revivalists have either dismissed or misunderstood their spiritual children. Very often, the biggest resistance toward a new season of revival has come from leaders and pioneers of the previous one. At the same time, the new and upcoming generations of spiritual leaders have often rejected the experience and wisdom of their fathers. This pattern is a terrible curse that the enemy has placed on the body of Christ. But Jesus broke this cursed pattern on the cross and has made us into one new man in Christ. In fact, the Old Testament ends with this very powerful promise of restoration between the generations:

Behold, I will send you Elijah the prophet before the coming of the great and dreadful day of the Lord. And he will turn the hearts of the fathers to the children and the hearts of the children to their fathers, lest I come and strike the earth with a curse (Mal. 4:5-6 NKJV).

These verses are the last passage of the Old Testament and they describe the anointing and mandate of Elijah. It is no coincidence that already at the beginning of the New Testament, these verses are being quoted again. The angel Gabriel refers to these verses when speaking about John the Baptist's ministry as a forerunner: *"And it is he who will go as a forerunner before Him in the spirit and power of Elijah, to turn the hearts of fathers back to their children and the disobedient to the attitude of the righteous, to make ready a people prepared for the Lord" (Luke 1:17 NASB).* John the Baptist operated in the anointing of Elijah, as he prepared the way for the coming of Christ. We will also minister in this anointing to prepare for His return in glory.

The Anointing of Elijah

The body of Christ will operate in the ministry and anointing of Elijah to prepare the second coming of Christ. As the return of Jesus is drawing nearer, this ministry will be restored in a much greater way than we have ever seen before, even since the day of Pentecost. Powerful reconciliation and miracles of healing and restoration will take place between the fathers and sons. This will bring deep healing, even to the deepest wounds in the body of Christ, so that we can live in the fullness of divine life. Malachi gives us a promise of this in the same prophecy that we just read. *"But for you who fear My name, the sun of righteousness will rise with healing in its wings; and you will go forth and frolic like calves from the stall" (Mal. 4:2 NASB).* Abraham operated powerfully in this anointing, which was one of the main reasons that Isaac became such a fruitful and blessed man. Let's pray for the Father to pour out this anointing once again upon the body of Christ. To have a father's heart toward spiritual sons means to hope and pray that coming generations will become even more fruitful and blessed than our generation. To have the heart of a son towards spiritual parents means to want to help in fulfilling their dreams. This will be one of the fruits of a deeper revelation of the Father's heart. It is by abiding in His love that spiritual sons and fathers are being formed and released into the world.

Activations

- In this chapter, we have studied how Abraham found a bride for Isaac. This story is a powerful picture of Christ and the bride. Study this story together with Jesus. You'll find it in Gen. 24:1-67. Invite the Holy Spirit to give deep revelation about the bride of the Lamb. Write down any new revelation you receive.

- We are called to pass on blessings and breakthroughs to the next generation. Take time to reflect on your spiritual inheritance. What blessings and treasures are the most important ones for you to pass on to the people you train and invest in? List the three most important ones.

- Take 20-30 minutes in prayer. Ask the Father to connect you to the people that you are called to raise up in Christ and train. Ask Him to give you the grace and wisdom to multiply what He has given to you in many brothers and sisters in Christ.

- Take some time in intercession for the body of Christ. There are two important things to pray for that come into my mind when writing this chapter:

  1. *Pray for the bride of the Lamb to be made ready and for us to grow in our bridal identity.*

  2. *Pray for the anointing and mandate of Elijah to come upon us in even greater measures. Ask for the restoration between fathers and sons and for generational blessings to be passed on among us.*

Pray and intercede over these prayer requests. Some of you will get prophetic words, or deeper revelation of the bride of Christ while you pray. Write down these words.

CLOSING WORDS

We have now come to the end of this book and I hope that you've been blessed by reading it. I surely had a good time writing these pages. I always find it very humbling to study or write about the riches and treasures of our sonship and identity in Christ. The treasures we have in Christ are truly more precious than we can even begin to understand. You are a carrier of the presence of God and your life is filled with all of heaven's blessings. You are called to spread the love of the Father everywhere and to extend His Kingdom. Making it your life's purpose to spread His love, will set you up for a very rich and exciting life. You are called to live as a child of God, who moves forward with the heavenly vision in bold faith. This is the lifestyle that Jesus modeled for us:

I speak to you eternal truth. The Son is unable to do anything from himself or through his own initiative. I only do the works that I see the Father doing, for the Son does the same works as his Father. Because the Father loves his Son so much, he always reveals to him everything that he is about to do. And you will all be amazed when he shows him even greater works than what you've seen so far (John 5:19-20 TPT).

This statement from Jesus about His relationship with the Father, reveals what it means to live in Christlikeness and sonship. You are invited to live from the Father's heart, rooted and grounded in His love. This is the pathway, both to fruitfulness and restful increase.

Your Notes from the Activations

If you have been doing the activations at the end of every chapter while reading this book, you have a journal with the revelations the Holy Spirit has given to you. I suggest that you spend some time after you have finished this book to read and pray over these revelations. They are the Father's revelations to you, His beloved and favored child. I'm confident that you will be amazed at how much He has revealed to you through these activations. Maybe they even have provided material for you to write your own book?

Your Life and Vision Matters

I'm fully convinced that you will follow Abraham's example and be blessed with a long and satisfying life. You have been destined to bear a lot of lasting fruit and the Lord will use you to impact the lives of multitudes of people. The Father loves you and He has planned a very exciting future for you. You will live a long and fruitful life together with the Father. What you're building for God right now will have a greater impact upon this world than you can imagine. Your vision is important, because within it, there is potential to reach thousands of people with the love of the Father. This is the reason that Satan tries to discourage you and make you quit. His worst nightmare is that you would start walking in your full inheritance as a favored child of God. Your life matters much more than you know. It is important to grasp that when we respond to the Father by living in the vision that He has given, people's lives will be transformed by the power of Jesus. The Kingdom of God is growing in this world through the people who respond to His calling.

You Are a Blessing

I have written this book to encourage you to break free from all religious boxes and traditions of man that have held you back. The reason why this is so very important is that religion will steal your potential and kill your dreams, but that is not your destiny. You have been blessed to be a blessing to this world. You possess the abundant life of heaven and you have inherited the Kingdom of God. You have been destined to break through into new areas so that the Kingdom of God can grow and increase through you.

You have been called to see hundreds of people saved, delivered and healed by the love of the Father. The Father loves the world and He wants to express His love through you. As you abide in His love, it will compel you to overcome every challenge, so that you can be and do everything that the Father has called you to be and do.

Your best days are ahead of you. The life of Jesus will be revealed through you like never before. You are a blessing to this world! I want to end this book by once again reminding you of the most important thing: *Your Father loves you and He is well-pleased with you!*

"The grace of the Lord Jesus Christ and the love of God and the communion of the Holy Ghost, be with you all. Amen" (2 Cor 13:14).

BIBLIOGRAPHY

Strong, James. *Strong's Exhaustive Concordance of the Bible.* Peabody: Hendrickson Publishers, 2009.

Unless otherwise indicated, all scriptural quotations are from the *King James Version* of the Bible.

Scripture references marked AMP are taken from Amplified® Bible Copyright © 2015 by The Lockman Foundation, La Habra, CA 90631.

Scripture references marked The Message are taken from The Message. Copyright © 1993, 1994, 1995, 1996, 2000, 2001, 2002.

Scripture references marked NASB are taken from NEW AMERICAN STANDARD BIBLE® NASB® Copyright © 1960, 1971, 1977,1995, 2020 by The Lockman Foundation A Corporation Not for Profit La Habra, CA. All Rights Reserved.

Scripture references marked NIV are taken from the HOLY BIBLE, NEW INTERNATIONAL VERSION®. NIV®. Copyright © 1973, 1978, 1984 by the International Bible Society.

Scripture quotations marked NLT are taken from the Holy Bible, New Living Translation, copyright 1996, 2004, 2007, 2015 by Tyndale House Foundation. Used by permission of Tyndale House Publishers, Inc., Carol Stream, Illinois 60188. All rights reserved.

Scripture references marked NKJV are taken from The Holy Bible, New King James Version, Copyright © 1982 Thomas Nelson. All rights reserved.

Scripture references marked TPT are taken from The Passion Translation® is a registered trademark of Passion and Fire Ministries, Inc. Copyright © 2020 Passion and Fire Ministries, Inc.

About the Author

Martin Reén lives in the north of Sweden together with His wife Linda and their children Isak, Benjamin and Noomi. Martin's and Linda's vision has always been to grow in knowing the heart of the Father in deeper ways, as well as to grow in intimacy with Jesus Christ and daily be more conformed into His image. They want to introduce as many parts of the body of Christ as possible to the Father's love and the finished work of Jesus Christ, so that believers can be secure in their identity as sons and daughters and live by the life of Christ. Martin and Linda travel all over the world to preach the gospel and teach in Bible schools, seminars, conferences and on-line events. They also work with missions, counselling and leadership training.